T0328518

Reflections on Labour
and
Trade Unions

Other titles

Reflections on Industry and Economy
Reflections on Media and Gender Issues
Reflections on Good Governance and Democracy
Reflections on African and Global Affairs
Reflections on Friends, Comrades and Heroes

Reflections on Labour and Trade Unions

Issa Aremu

malthouse $\overline{\mathcal{M}P}$

Malthouse Press Limited

Lagos, Benin, Ibadan, Jos,Port-Harcourt, Zaria

© Issa Aremu 2015
First published 2015
ISBN 978-978-53321-2-4

Malthouse Press Limited
43 Onitana Street, Off Stadium Hotel Road,
Off Western Avenue, Lagos Mainland
E-mail: malthouse_press@yahoo.com
malthouselagos@gmail.com
Tel: +234 (01) 0802 600 3203

Foreword

As may be expected of any columnist reacting to events, decisions, and prevailing circumstances occurring over a reasonable number of years, it should not be surprising that Issa Aremu followed no particular order in his treatment of matters he has grouped broadly under "Labour and Trade Unions".

On much the same grounds, I suggest little attention be paid to the evaluative term "Reflections", which forms part of the title of this book, a good many of the write-ups in their nature being in the heat of the moment reaction by him, not to add generally notorious and punishing deadlines imposed on columnists by slave-driving editors!

Even if all that were true, the contents of this rich collection of write-ups by Issa Aremu also reveal evidence of some reflection that an impossible deadline for submission of an article should leave unscathed; putting any disparate views together on any one subject matter involves some reflection by definition.

I think Issa has demonstrated admirable competence in his dissection of an astonishing variety of claims and counter-claims while confronting matters in respect of: i) governments' labour and employment policies; ii) likely and actual impacts of certain strands of governments' economic policies – like structural adjustment measures; iii) challenges of labour law and legislative authorities; iv) poorly thought-through compensation and wage policies; v) challenges facing union organization, especially institution-building and solidarity; vi) mass employment and mass unemployment; vii) standard of living of working people; viii) pension schemes and their administration; ix) industrial conflict and strikes over perennial increases in prices of imported refined petroleum products and in the educational and medical sectors especially; and x) coverage of industrial relations and trade unionism in the print media.

In all, like Issa Aremu shows convincingly, given the centrality of formal training and education to modern life and nation-building, it remains puzzling why teachers at all levels remain poorly paid and feel the need to go on incessant strikes; why doctors and nurses have to embark upon strike actions for salaries and allowances to be properly calibrated and administered; legislators and politicians wring their hands as hard-earned pensions of pensioners get brazenly embezzled; a minimum wage that can hardly cover transport to and from places of work in the urban areas where most workers may be found; and why one of the world's largest producers of crude oil and gas retains a policy, for over thirty years, of non-functioning refineries and importation of refined petroleum products and subject the trade unions and citizens to periodic bouts of nation-wide protests to "agree" rate at which a litre of diesel, kerosene and petrol respectively be sold for; and, all this and more, while criticizing levels of workers' and national productivity.

Then in tow is a mish-mash of critics, often difficult to separate into ever-present government apologists, hatchet-persons for local and foreign intelligence organisations pushing one narrative or the other, and die-hard anti-unionists who attribute all ills in work relations to the trade unions and "radicals" they would rather see "bought" or, failing that, "destroyed" on pages of newspapers.

I have enjoyed reading all the write-ups in this book, in spite of the inescapable picture of parlous and substantially conflict-ridden state of labour and employment relations in the country which they press forcefully on one. One industry, though, which seems to have escaped Issa Aremu's periscope is the banking and finance industry where mounting evidence points to a host of recent human resource management practices tending to re-define the law of contract and are substantially at variance with Nigerian labour law and ignore the core conventions of the International Labour Organization. Happy reading!

Dafe Otobo, DPhil (Oxford)
University of Lagos, Akoka-Yaba

Table of contents

- Labour Under SAP - **1**
- Labour According to the Media - **5**
- Unions not for Sale - **8**
- What About the Workers? - **11**
- Crisis of Compensation - **14**
- Crisis of Productivity - **18**
- What About the Unionists? - **21**
- Restoring Trade Union Independence - **26**
- End of Work (I) - **30**
- Wage Crisis: A Nigerian Paradox - **34**
- Labour and Development - **38**
- Obasanjo: Labour Dimension – **43**
- Labour and Development II - **45**
- Life After Work - **50**
- Labour and Democratic Process - **55**
- Pension Act of 2004: Labour Dimension - **59**
- End of Work (II) - **63**
- Human (Re)Capitalisation - **66**
- Pope John Paul II: Labour Dimension - **69**
- Re-thinking Labour -I - **72**
- Pensions: Beyond Verification - **76**
- May Day and 2007 Polls - **79**
- Strike as an Acid Test - **83**
- Re-inventing Decent Mass Employment - **86**
- Teachers' Strike and Servant Leadership - **90**
- NIS Recruitment Tragedy or Unemployment Tsunami - **94**

- Pay Cut or Pay Equity? - **98**
- Labour as Endangered Species - **102**
- ILO @ 90 - **105**
- NSITF: Building Social Floor for Workers - **108**
- Minimum Wage, Minimum Delay - **111**
- How Productive is Nigeria? - **14**
- 10th NLC Delegates' Conference - **118**
- Wanted Emergency on Job Creation - **122**
- Understanding the New Employees Compensation Act - **125**
- NECO; Mass Failure or Poorly Motivated Teachers? - **129**
- Fuel Price Protest; Matters Arising - **133**
- Union Makes Us Strong (I) - **136**
- Union Makes Us Strong (II) - **140**
- Pension Fraud; What about the Pensioners? - **144**
- Doctors' Sack: End of Decent Work - **147**
- ASUU; In Praise of Institution Building - **150**
- Centenary of Nigerian Labour Movement - **153**
- Rethinking Labour II - **156**
- Nigeria: In Defence of Pension Assets - **159**
- Abdulrasheed Maina, In Praise of the Senate - **162**
- Saving the Pensioners - **166**
- Africa's Premier Trade Union, OATUU at 40 - **169**
- Towards the ILO Centenary - **173**
- Nigeria; Amending the Pension Act - **177**
- Rethinking Senate Constitution Amendment on Labour- **180**
- ASUU Strike: Crisis of Collective Bargaining - **184**
- What About Industrial Relations? - **187**
- What About Industrial Relations II? - **191**
- Building Up Workers' Power: 3rd ITUC World Congress- **194**
- Africa Special Pension Summit - **198**
- Rethinking the Doctors' Mass Sack - **201**
- The 2014 National Productivity Day - **204**
- Reinventing the Human Resource - **207**

About the Author

Comrade Issa Obalowu Aremu, NPOM, mni, was born in 1961 to the extended family of Mallam Mahmood Aremu and Hadjia Afusat Amoke of Alapata and Kasandubu compounds of Ilorin respectively. He attended Ansar Ud Deen primary school, Ijagbo. He had his secondary education at Ilorin Grammar School before moving to School of Basic Studies, Ahmadu Bello University, ABU, Zaria in 1977.

Issa's passion for organizing and activism started in the late 1970s and early 80s, decades of progressive and radical ideas in ABU. He was an active member of ABU students' unionism and rose to become the Secretary General of the reputable radical Marxist-Leninist Movement for Progressive Nigeria (MPN). He was among the score of students' leaders repressed with expulsion by Ango Abdullahi Vice Chancellorship in 1981 at his final year. He eventually obtained his BSc (Hons) degree in Economics from University of Port Harcourt in 1985 with Second Class Upper. He has his Master degree in Labour and Development studies from the prestigious Institute for Social Studies (ISS), The Hague, The Netherlands, in 1991. He is an alumnus of George Meany Labour Centre, Maryland, Washington, USA (1987 and 2003). He joined the labour movement as the Head, Economic/Research department of Nigeria Labour Congress (NLC) between 1987 and 1989. He later moved to the National Union of Textile Garment and Tailoring Workers of Nigeria (NUTGTWN), a private sector affiliate union of NLC in 1989. After 20 years of active union carrier, he rose from an organizing Secretary to become the General Secretary of the union in March 2000. He took over as the General Secretary of the union from Comrade Adams Oshiomhole, mni, the Comrade governor of Edo State and two times former President of Nigeria Labour Congress (NLC).

Comrade Issa Aremu is currently one of the Vice-Presidents of the Nigeria Labour Congress (NLC). In 2013 In Johannesburg, South Africa, he was elected the Chairman, new IndustriALL Global Union, Africa Region with more than 50 million members in 165 countries with headquarters in Geneva, Switzerland making an Executive African Member of IndustriALL Global Union. Having attended Senior Executive Course 27 of the National Institute (mni) for Policy and Strategic Studies, Kuru, Jos in 2005, Comrade Issa Aremu is a Member of the National Institute.

In 2013 he was elected the Secretary-General of the Alumni Association of the National Institute for Policy & Strategy Studies, AANI.

He is currently the Chairman of the Interim Management Committee of First Guarantee Pension Limited and a member of the tripartite National Labour Advisory Committee (NLAC) made up of government, employers and trade unions. He also serves in the Board of Labour City Transport Service (LCTS). He is the Chairman, International Committee of Nigeria Labour Congress (NLC).

Comrade Issa Aremu, mni, has served on the Board of Michael Imoudu National Institute of Labour Studies (MINILS) and Nigeria Social Insurance Trust Fund (NSITF). His contributions helped to reposition these institutions as leading labour market institutions in Nigeria. He had served on the tripartite Federal National Minimum Wage, in 2000 and 2010 and Petroleum Products Pricing Regulatory Committee in 2003 as well as tripartite committee on Revival of textile and Garment industry. He has led negotiations and signed hundreds of national collective agreements on salaries, allowances, gratuity and pensions of textile, garment and tailoring workers over the years.

A visible leading member of mass national actions on socio-political issues during the struggle for democracy and against military dictatorship in the 1980s and 1990s, Comrade Issa is a weekly columnist with Abuja-based, *Daily Trust* newspapers. His published works include; *The Social Relevance of Trade Unionism, The Crises of Pricing Petroleum Products in Nigeria, Collapse of Textile Industry in Nigeria: Implications for Employment and Poverty Eradication and Tears Not Enough.*

Comrade Issa Aremu, mni was one of the labour delegates to the 2014 National Conference. He was the Deputy Chairman of the National Conference Committee on Civil Society, Labour, Youth and Sports. He is a strong activist and advocate on, Redistribution of national wealth, improved Productivity and Re-Industrialisation of Nigerian economy. Recipient of many distinguished awards and recognitions, the President of Nigeria, Dr. Goodluck Ebele Jonathan, GCFR, on August 21, 2014 in recognition of his contribution to national productivity improvement and consciousness conferred on him the National Productivity Order of Merit (NPOM) Award. He is married with children.

Labour Under SAP*

"Capital should be at the service of labour and not labour at the
service of capital."
- *Pope John Paul II*

It was quite interesting reading the informed article of Odia Ofeimun in The *Guardian* edition of July 3. Indeed, the article may well be the most objective assessment of the celebrated Structural Adjustment Programme (SAP). It did not only establish the fact that the component parts of the programme are mutually destructive (witness a ban on new banks at Foreign Exchange Market (FEM) bidding sessions and even "return" of the removed petroleum subsidy via the second window), but quite correctly, Ofeimun showed that SAP, so far, is a burden on the people.

Emphasis on the word "people", because, it is a nebulous word or concept. Remember the politicians' people, which in the main are, ghost voters, or coup-plotters' "citizenry" which is non-existent. Nobody certainly can doubt Ofeimun's conception of people. In that article, his point of departure was stridently patriotic and his sense of purpose was well true to character: humanistic. But this fact can only be brought to the fore, if we remove area of doubt and avoid terms that could make imagination run riot. How for instance, have wage-earners and their dependants fared under the heels of SAP in the past one year?

Dr. Nnamdi Azikiwe once told *The Guardian* that the defunct SFEM sounded "Greek" and quite in keeping with the simplicity of the aged and their wisdom, he added: It is a clear devaluation of our currency". If SFEM sounded "Greek" to our great Zik, it is clear

---

* *The Guardian*, 9th July 1986

that semi-skilled, great mass of unskilled and not a few skilled wage-earners are indeed in deplorable conditions. SFEM was beyond the comprehension of wage-earners. It was doubtful whether trade unions were invited to the first ever organised Finance Fair where we were told, a mock bidding session was held.

Never before has wage-income come under a vicious attack. Curiously enough, while the "new" bankers were casualties of what they campaigned for, that is, 'market forces', workers were held hostages of what they did not bargain for. While SAP was to ostensibly usher in an era of deregulated economy, it has simply ignored the hated yearly guideline of the Productivity, Prices and Incomes Board (PPIB) which arrogantly imposes wage freeze. Workers were simply not allowed to collectively bargain for their worth, even if their price will be instinctively dubbed "unrealistic" by the experts. Herein lies one injustice of SAP. It has not allowed for wage increase even when high prices of goods and profits of banks and big companies are being presented as articles of faith.

We have been repeatedly told about the need to let the "tail wag the dog", such as allowing international prices to dictate domestic prices. True, the second-tier exchange rates had merged at ₦3.9500 to one dollar, but a conspiracy of silence persists on what this means to a minimum wage earner. What is the dollar value of ₦125 minimum wage? What happens to the purchasing power?

Even more important is that against the backdrop of naira devaluation and wage freeze, such dishonest terms as "consumer resistance" or "buyers market" had been evoked to explain an alleged reduction in prices. But workers know that they cannot resist what they have no alternatives for – basic needs. Nor can they lay claim to a market at which their "sovereignty" has been limited by reduced pay. The executive director of Manufacturers' Association of Nigeria (MAN), Dr. Fafowora recently disclosed that most workers survive today because they engage in 'moonlighting'. Hmmm...I should have known that.

One veritable appeal of SFEM enlightenment campaign committee is that "government revenue will be enhanced" via the second-window. This is the workers' "promissory" note. Yet it took Bendel State civil servants a week-long protracted strike to convince

2

Colonel John Inienger, it seems, before rushing to Lagos to obtain N76 million for the payment of outstanding allowances directed by 1987 budget. Also not long ago, Colonel Ahmed Abdullahi was on "Kwara's wage bill mission to Lagos" amidst scandalous report that the state was "broke". Certainly it requires no serious argument to support workers' demand to know what happens to government revenue (they pay taxes and produce) than to consent to the belated request of bankers for increased government funding of SFEM. More so, when virtually all the states were in festivity during the month of May. What happens to workers' "promissory notes"?

And talking about petroleum subsidy, Mr. Rilwanu Lukman, the Energy Minister recently said with SFEM "we are back to where we started." SAP's instruments may be mutually elusive after all. But workers have been forced to pay higher prices for this officially confirmed anarchistic programme. For one, every commuter knows that the increase in fares predates the recently announced increases by Nigerian Transporters' Association. Hitherto, it was true, the increases were not announced but there were increases nonetheless. Where transporters did not openly announce increases in fares, they cut short routes and charged double fares, thus the latest approved increases constitute a bitter insult to a deep and painful injury.

Much has been said (albeit orchestrated) about maintenance culture. It is perfectly correct for equipment and machines to be renewed and retouched. But what happens to human resources? Can't they be maintained too? Thanks to SAP-induced high production costs, workers in the factories now bear the burden of obnoxious "cost-effective" measures. Where computerization has not led to retrenchment, employers simply disregard the orders of arbitration panels. Directors find it convenient to declare meagre dividends than to announce how many workers they have trained in the year ended. SFEM has become a veritable excuse for ever mean Nigerian employers. Worse still, workers cannot afford prohibitive education bills for themselves and their children. Thus a significant section of the society has been condemned to ignorance, same for its offspring.

And, may we know how industrial relations have been under the regime of SAP? More than ever before, most employers have become notorious union bashers.

Yet the real issue today is not what workers are doing to alleviate their conditions, but that there exists a group of fanatical "believers" who still disbelieve the above obvious facts: that SAP equals "sadism as praxis". Herein lies the danger for the future. Crude and insidious doctrine has been substituted for reason and social justice.

Labour according to the media[*]

Not long ago, the Lagos State Chief Executive, Governor Mike Akhigbe mooted a suggestion that states should adopt differentiated wage-structures. Definitely there was nothing new about Governor Akhigbe's suggestion given that government dating back to colonial times and mostly in the wake of inability to fulfil the basic obligation of salary payment often mooted desperate options out of the crisis. But what is 'new' about the recent suggestion of the Governor is the unusual manner the media celebrated it, even as belated as it were. We were told by those who perhaps would want to be counted for financial sagacity, that differentiated wage structure would reduce the burden of wage-bill for the states and even the Federal Government. It was not clear how this conclusion was arrived at, but one notable theoretical justification can be found in the opinion of the Guardian columnist, Chief Effiong Essien published in April 1987.

In this article, the columnist advocated a kind of 'group-area' wage-rates that would perhaps 'modernize' the discredited colonial Miller wage-grouping of 1940s. True to logic, argument for wage zonalisation rests on such unscientific and absurd premises as differentiated eating habits of the diverse people of Nigeria.

Indeed, the columnist tried to argue that zonal wage structure enhances labour mobility, reflects differentiated costs of living and consequently would efficiently allocate resources, among other things.

Strikingly enough discussion on the need to adopt a non-uniform wage payment for full work done came at a time a co-ordinated plan (through obnoxious decrees) to kill the national

- *National Concord*, Thursday 5th October, 1987 pg 3

5

minimum wage structure was uncovered. Thus the idea of differentiated wage structure came simultaneously with the National Minimum Wage Order of 1986 which chose to erode the gains the workers had won through the hard way as far back as 1981. Even at the same time too, the Governors (undoubtedly by default) had also been bestowed (to the bargain) with Decree 38 which gave them the emergency power to deduct workers' pay ostensibly for development.

It is important to point out that the proponents of zonal (as distinct from national) wage structure largely often rest their views on anything but fairness and social justice. Any attempt to differentiate wage structure on the state basis would violate the principle of "Equal Pay for Equal Work". It is capable of hindering the workers' struggle for a living wage on a national scale.

A version of this divisive and exploitative wage structure in recent times is the notorious IMO formula, which chose to pay civil servants according to the available revenue. Needless to say that the formula makes mockery of conditions of service and tenure, it casts ominous shadow on industrial relations. No wonder after a brief spell of its arbitrary implementation in Imo State, it faced fierce resistance of the workers in Niger under Governor Mark and it got consequently terminated in Imo State, its very testing ground.

However, more important is the latest erroneous impression being promoted in the media that wage increase if won, will become a harbinger of inflation. A 'labour journalist,' Umoh James Umoh wrote under the demagogic banner 'Wage Increase Amidst Inflation' (*Daily Times*, September 15, 1987). He did not only maliciously and erroneously attribute the NLC memo on wage increase to the "leaders of the Civil Service Technical Workers' Union", but also held workers and their organisations responsible for the economic crises. Yet anti-labour writers are yet to establish a link between wage adjustment and possible price rise beyond headlines that consciously nurture speculation and price riot. Thus the labour movement has chosen to disbelieve 'the obvious' according to these writers. When the Federal Ministry of Information, for instance, initiated a pet campaign 'against rising cost of living' it was an acknowledgement of rising prices even without wage increases. The slogan: "If it is too expensive, don't buy" did not identify consumers as culprits but manufacturers who in pursuit of profits maintain high prices side by side the pile ups in their ware houses. Even then, the beg-thy-neighbour policy of the government on inflation has been shown to be ill-fated. But will it really be correct to say wage increase would fuel inflation?

Answer to this question can only be proffered within the context of the present adjustment process. The thrust of SAP is deregulation. It means in policy measures terms, dismantling price controls, allowing for increases in fares and of late, hike in the cost of borrowing i.e. interest rates. Thus, undoubtedly, SAP nurtures inflation as its article of fate. It presumes it rational and normal. One then wonders why in a deregulated environment, wage freeze should be entertained. It is on this double-standard the critics of wage adjustment rest their claims.

Even then for the wage earner, a discussion on whether wages increase or not is largely academic. A worker needs definitely wage increase to cushion the effects of ever-rising prices and contend with deteriorating living conditions. Further, a serious labour observer ought to know that in the private sector for instance, end of services benefits of workers are often calculated on the wage-levels and not fringe benefits and allowances. Thus, in a society without social security, wage adjustment is a long term imperative for the working class. It is unfortunate that some writers rather than address this fundamental issue opted for petty subterfuge and divisive methods to split the labour movements. Witness the lead stories about "power tussle in the NLC" and "NLC plans to go ahead to form left party." It was Dan Agbese, a leading Nigerian journalist, who recently wrote that: "It has never crossed my mind how much pain and anguish the average Nigerian journalist brings on others." "Out of sheer laziness," he added, "I however thought much has to do with blackmail. Labour according to the media, confirms this thinking."

Unions Not For Sale[*]

Chief Bisi Onabanjo (read: Aiyekoto) in a recent television programme: "The Press", gave two reasons for his love for writing.

One, he said, is the irresistible urge for deliberate mischief and the other, self-indulgence for want of what to do. Well before this sincere, but mischievous disclosure by the Columnist, as a reader, I have always been weary of 'journalism by opinion and commentaries'. Weary because, often I feel I am being compelled to read the printed prejudices of some few writers on issues that require painstaking explanation and enlightenment. Indeed, my frustration is more with 'journalists', non-resident or guest writers than with information reports of journalists on the beats.

The government decision to dissolve the Executive organ of the 10-year old Nigeria Labour Congress (biggest of such centres in Africa!), has provoked interesting comments. True to character, columnists, being parrots that can talk it out, (labour is never their area of specialization) were not left out either. But, so far, two of these comments – I found most repulsive on the ground that they were not only uninformative but disgustingly in bad taste. They are: 'Unions for Sale' by Godwin Sogolo (*Guardian*, 7/3/88) and 'The crisis in Central Labour' by Pat Utomi (*Business Concord*, 11/3/88). These two write-ups have much in common; they were borne out of mischief, malice and self-indulgence, being the bane of columnists Chief Onabanjo rightly identified. This is bad enough because this is the time people want to be informed about the labour movement and not to inherit anybody's prejudices.

---

[*] *National Concord*, Thursday 12th May, 1988 pg. 3

First the mischief: Sogolo's choice of cited allegations and counter-allegations by individuals in the Congress as evidence of proven corruption of unions is certainly not helpful. For the author to say the outcome of Benin Quadrennial Conference of the NLC was a disagreement over 'exploits' was to lead readers by the nose. As a matter of fact reports by correspondents in Benin never reported 'exploits'. And when Sogolo said Congress' leaders "go, cap in hand, year after year demanding money from state government to hold conferences," he must have been ill-informed because conferences are never held yearly and no government has said it was being hosted, annually. Interesting enough, he also saw Congress leaders as 'labour aristocrats'. But nothing usual about this characterization. In December, when Mallam Yusuf Mamman, Press Secretary to Chief of General Staff, said NLC leaders, were 'aristocrats', it was not over proven 'exploits' but a desperate reaction to the Congress' agitation on 'petroleum subsidy'. Certainly Sogolo has the 'fundamental human right' to support the appointment of an administrator for the labour movement, no less than countless careerist-writers would support coup-plotters because civilians "are corrupt". Readers however know who is more corrupt. But Sogolo cannot act as the administrator (whose terms of reference, we were told include a probe into allegation of financial impropriety), on the pages of newspapers. Indeed it will be untenable to cheaply smear the unions, based on recent developments within the Congress. This is also why the decision of the government to make 'capital out of such cheap case' by dissolving the Congress should provoke question from right thinking observers than opportunistic commentary. Does the government have a moral and judicial ground to intervene in unions? So far, was it an intervention or taking side with some fifth columnists cultivated by the very government in the first place? Does the government feel "safer" without a central labour given that it has arrested labour leaders twice on the ground of unproven 'subversion'? Is the government committed to a 'virile' labour centre during adjustment programme which labour has singled out as source of all woes? Does the government that set corrupt politicians loose have the basis to probe union accounts which as a matter of

9

principle, it does not contribute to? What is the implication of the occupation of the secretariat of the Congress by armed policemen, for the promised transition in 1992? Some of these thought-provoking questions featured in the commendable and timely editorial of the *Guardian* on this issue. (See 'Crisis in Labour', 7/3/88). Sogolo should know that a good writer must learn to disbelieve the 'obvious', be critical and not as 'cynical' on issues with such a far-reaching implications for our corporate existence.

Business Concord columnist, Pat Utomi, who also wrote on the NLC crises conveyed same cynicism other then genuine concern. Thus while rightly recognizing that 'labour bashing' dominates public discourse, even saw the dissolution of the Congress as sad, he still went ahead to prescribe an environment without unions. According to him, workers are largely responsible for the lack of the country's growth because of their poor attitude to work and non-co-operationist unionism, allegedly imported from Europe. Quite in the tradition of World Bank and IMF model-building, Pat Utomi said: "Nigerian workers must be like Korean workers in 'efficient work culture." 'Unfortunately,' he added further, 'what we have is labour that has not given much thought to the common destiny of both worker and the owner in an economy such as ours which is much troubled.' Thus in an attempt to justify the dissolution of the Congress, Utomi had to revisit those clichés anybody can be 'convinced' on at endless seminars, namely, 'productivity, growth and the role of labour'. What an indulgence of a columnist.

Anybody with a deep knowledge of the labour movement will however realise that the attack on workers and their unions, now a commonplace, was once a national disgrace. Curiously enough, that was when colonial 'masters' saw even paramount chiefs as 'servants' and workers as 'boys'. What could have then happened to our sense of history?

What about the Workers?[*]

Wage-earners are increasingly confronted with unfair labour practices which directly erode their income and freely deny them their jobs altogether. Agonizing labour practices now constitute the rule in the public sector groaning under the heel of military government of varying persuasion. On the occasion of May Day, it is certainly a sad commentary that salary cut, non-payment of salary and job denials are now common features of work-relations. What is clearly worrisome is the fact that there seems to be no end to these unacceptable but recurring labour practices under the military.

We all can recall the indiscriminate retrenchment of workers following the military intervention in 1984. The Labour Act of 1974 provides that facts and circumstances of termination must necessarily be fair. But in an attempt to render this protective legislation irrelevant, Decree 16 & 17 of 1984 made termination an unchallengeable labour practice in court. Countless workers fell victims of this prohibitive ouster decrees.

Labour observers would also remember how all well-known notions of compensation and reward system were upturned and trampled. Remember the notorious Imo Formula according to which workers' monthly salary would be tied to (non)available revenue.

In 1985, the then governor of Niger State Col. David Mark, did not only cut salaries of civil servants arbitrarily but demanded that minimum wage provision be removed from the federal list. Ten years after, it is interesting to note that the Niger State Administrator tended to look back at Mark's discredited legacy with ironic nostalgia.

---

[*] *New Nigeria* newspapers, Monday 1st May, 1995 pg. 5

What with his improved version of Imo Formula by which the workers of the state were recently forced to sign an agreement to which they were not party and an agreement which fell short of federal governments announced relief package.

The state military administrator also reportedly promised that labour matters in the state would henceforth be summarily addressed in such a military way. "Niger Formula", defined as jackboot industrial relations, has long been applied in Benue, Borno and Cross River states by their respective military administrators with no less disastrous effect on workers.

But the latest version of intolerable labour practices being enacted in Ilorin proves an ugly exception to already deplorable rule. "Kwara Formula" combines all unfair practices with something more sinister and iniquitous: security-hunt for unionists, mass termination and dissolution of workers' unions. This is in addition to the fact that promised 100 per cent increase in rent and transport was cut to 50 per cent.

What is however remarkable is the mute indifference to the tragedy that has befallen public employees in most states of the federation. No discernible policy statement yet from the Federal Ministry of Labour about the desirability or otherwise of labour practices in most states. When the Federal Government announced its relief package it was meant to "cushion" the effects of 238 per cent increase in the price of petrol and other petroleum products. Do the state administrators have discretion to pay favoured rates on account of "dwindling revenue" even when they collected federal grant to help them meet this end?

Are state employees less affected by the harsh economic crisis than their counterparts in the federal and private sectors? How valid is the argument of 'inability to pay' in such states as Kwara with dishonourable record of resource-diversion and sheer mismanagement? Are states' civil servants also citizens of corporate Nigeria? Or should we keep on treating them as some besieged and harassed refugees of some Bantustan home-lands who deserve nothing more than token relief measures?

Does sharp differential in remuneration not have adverse effects on workers' morale, labour mobility, productivity, and national unity?

In what way does the cause of industrial peace and harmony advanced with whimsical dissolution of unions and arrest of trade unionists pursuing their legitimate economic interest as required by labour laws? These questions certainly beg for answers.

The Sole Administrator of NLC, Mr. Ason Bur, had bemoaned the dissolution of public sector unions in Kwara pointing out that industrial unions are part of federal and *not* state list. So much for the legal implications of industrial relations by military diktat! But if the actions of the state administrator vilify the federal constitution with impunity, has anybody reflected on the human dimension of their unfair labour practices? What about the workers who are at the receiving end of triple assaults of cut in benefit and wages, retrenchment and security hunt or denial of free association?

Perhaps we may for one consider the plight of that person suddenly and arbitrarily retrenched. If he or she is the breadwinner, it is clear then that the family support collapses. Food may be difficult to find to feed the children with all the implications for malnutrition. Some kids may be withdrawn from school on account of non-payment of school fees while Easter or Sallah cloth will necessarily elude them. Pray the family is not sick either. Since the breadwinner cannot meet expectation, depression logically replaces love within the household. The options before retrenched men and women in a society without social security like Nigeria are therefore better imagined.

The point is that in Nigeria, official hesitation must precede mass termination. May the knowledge and appreciation of the dire economic consequences of joblessness temper the current wave of unfair and inhuman labour practices in most states of the federation.

13

Crisis of Compensation*

The 1996 budget will put to test the real commitment of the Abacha administration to poverty alleviation. Nigeria is in a profound crisis of compensation. This crisis is assuming a tragic dispensation such that it deserves more attention than the political and human rights' crisis, which often dominate the media. While there may be lack of unity on political/human rights issue, there is almost a national consensus today that the wage system and reward system in general has collapsed. Behind almost all the strikes, which have hit all the sectors of the economy in recent time, is the crisis of compensation and declining purchasing power. The real threat to democratization process is the desperation of workers in the face of falling purchasing power and the attendant poverty. A hungry man will be less tolerant and less democratic. The crisis manifests itself in different forms of inequities, which characterize the compensation system in the country.

One notable inequity lies in the nominalization of wages as a result of the inequitable, social unjust and insensitive economic policies contained in the Structural Adjustment Programme (SAP). The first two years of SAP in Nigeria witnessed wage-freeze without price control. And in 1988, when the wage freeze gave way to active bargaining, the twin policies of naira devaluation and removal of subsidies on petroleum products had taken effects such that the price inflation far more exceeded the wage concessions. The result is that currency devaluation and diminished value of money depressed workers' real wage. Price inflation has effectively led to wage cut without the obvious dictate of the employers and the government.

---

* *National Concord*, Wednesday 24th January 1996, pg 21

Even in those few sectors where there have been aggressive bargaining, the monthly average earnings and minimum wage do not compensate for the loss of income as a result of price inflation.

The trend towards the sharp decline in wage income, however, contrasts with relative growing income that goes to other factors, notably capital. Herein lies another inequity in the reward system. There has been a shift in the distribution of income in favour of business and business owners as witnessed in the phenomenal increases in profits. On the average, the business owners have been able to pass on the costs to the customers, which also include workers. It means to the extent that industry declares profits, employers do actually profit from price inflation. This in turn underscores the gravity of the compensation crisis. When the return on investment is combined with profits and the generous allowances hidden and unhidden transfers available to the managerial and business classes are considered, it will be seen that in the real world, the rich is truly getting richer. The share of labour in the domestic factor income has been on the decline as the share capital has increased. Low employment income has further worsened the employment crisis. The miserable conditions of pensioners in recent times also added a new dimension to the crisis of reward for work. Pensioners in Nigeria truly constitute the new poor whose gratuity is either denied or paid when they are already dead. Lack of staff commitment to work may also be attributed to the prospects of helplessness after tenure.

Another discernible inequity in compensation is the growing gap between the public and the private sector pay. While there has been a sharp decline in the wage income of all categories of the work-force, it should be noted that the earnings of the public civil servants have witnessed a remarkable stagnation in the face of rising prices. For instance, after making an allowance for the mandatory deductions and taxes, the average monthly emolument for the low income workers (level 05 - 07) in the Federal public sector amounts to a meagre sum of ₦1,076.10. This compares to the average earnings of ₦3,500.00 for the same category of workers in the private sector. The futility of comparison between the two sectors is, however, underscored by the fact that the average earnings in the two sectors in 1994 fell below the estimate sum needed for bare subsistence of a family of typical low-income earners compiled by the trade unions in the same year. This means low-income earners suffer from acute deprivations and want because their wages cannot meet their basic needs.

All the above inequities in compensation explain the frustration and despair of the workers in the formal sector with all the adverse implications for the staff commitment to work and productivity in the economy. The challenge before the government, employers and the trade unions lies in overcoming these inequities.

The efforts towards economic recovery and even transition to civil rule will prove difficult unless there is an urgent resolution of the crisis of compensation confronting the economy. Only through wages can workers meet the basic necessities of life. This means it is imperative that workers demand equitable wages and incomes in general so as to meet the basic needs. High wages however have positive effects on the economic. In the context of Nigerian economy, high wages will ensure high level of effective demand for goods and services; especially now that most warehouses of companies are full of unsold goods due to depressed purchasing power. This will definitely assist in stimulating the economy as a whole. Thus it is not the workers who have vested interests in equitable wage incomes but the economy as a whole. There is therefore an urgent need for a radical review of the structure of existing compensation system before workers can be motivated and their commitment to work assured.

Returns on work must go beyond the present "tokenism" in forms of "relief packages". The slide towards relief as distinct from compensation for workers in Nigeria belies the claim of the country as the giant of Africa. 'Relief' is meant for refugees, (who are in the abundance in such countries as Liberia, Rwanda and Somalia) not workers whose commitment is needed for the dynamic economy such as Nigeria's. Motivational financial packages must therefore transcend a 'relief' and guarantee living conditions for the workers. Let's hope that the 1996 budget will come out with some creative ideas on how to transform the existing obsolete compensation order as well as make compensation system truly equitable.

Crisis of Productivity[*]

Today is Productivity Day. For once, we are called upon to reflect on an all-important issue, which ought to be everyday's pre-occupation anyway. Since 21st February was decreed a Productivity Awareness Day in 1987, activities on this day have assumed the infamous 'Nigerian' character; ceremonial, top-down and distinguishably non-value-added. Marked by award-peddling and related bloated activities, Productivity Day is proving a consummately affair, an end in itself; which is not to be so, if truly today should provide an opportunity to elicit an awareness about productivity.

The importance of productivity cannot be over-emphasized. Understandably, issues about human rights are now fashionable in Africa, just as issues dealing with human duties slide into disfavour. What with dictatorship of varying persuasions suffocating a sizeable proportion of the continent? Yet the truth must be told; after democratic question is resolved, what deliver the continent into prosperity is not the volumes of bills of rights elegantly drafted for its citizens but the quantities and qualities of goods and services creatively produced by its citizens. At the root of the problem in Africa is productivity issue and the truth is that little is being produced and poorly too.

Reviewing the World Bank's study of Africa's plight for 1989, the London *Economist* dubbed Africa 'The Bleak Continent.' Statistics convey the message better: Africa's 450 million produced almost as much as Belgium's only 10 million. In the 1980s, Africa's rate of return on investment reportedly collapsed to just 2½ per cent while that of South Asia increased by 22 per cent. In the 1990s, the

---

[*] *New Nigeria* newspapers, Wednesday 21st February 1996, pg 5

18

situation has even gone worse for Africa, as growth of GDP per worker has turned negative. In view of the fact that Belgium's productive capacity far more outweighs its absorptive capacity, Africa which produces below capacity automatically becomes a dumping ground for Belgium goods, albeit scandalously in second hand forms nowadays. The lesson here is that prosperity and poverty are functions of productivity.

What even makes Africa's productivity problem assume a crisis proportion is the distributional issues associated with it. The little that is produced is disproportionately shared in favour of the few who contribute little or no value. As politics of management gets acrimonious and turned crudely a 'zero-sum' game, the "haves" have gained more while the "have-nots" lose out and often lose out completely. Perhaps there is nowhere in the continent than Nigeria, where distribution issue manifests itself clearly given the abysmal low returns on work and efforts while idle non-productive class corners it all. Any attempt to induce productivity awareness which, in turn ignores the issue of distribution of even the little produced among its producers will not lead to desired results. Productivity problem is intricately linked with distribution problem.

In order to encourage production therefore, we must urgently motivate the work force. The motto of Nigeria Labour Congress is "Labour Creates Wealth". With this self-realisation, it is clear that Nigerian workers need no sermons on the need to produce more. One critical issue is that of creating "enabling environment" for the desired goal of increased productivity. Officially, the established National Productivity Centre (NPC) is charged with the responsibilities to work out among other things, productivity schemes which can motivate workers to 'produce more'. Definitely labour is not the only factor of production. Yet any productivity improvement effort which does not single out labour as a point of departure is defective. For one, labour is the most visible factor. Only labour has conscious control over its contribution to output and even the contribution of other production factors. All these factors underscore the need for labour to be accorded a special attention in discussing the issue of productivity.

Regrettably, labour has been condescendingly treated in our top-down and managerial perception of productivity, particularly since the inception of Structural Adjustment Programme (SAP). For instance, when we talk about "maintenance culture", as we often do, it readily comes to mind that we mean putting obsolete machinery and equipment back to work. But what happens to the human beings? It is an open knowledge that most enterprises and managers do not know what their costs are or how to cut them. Interestingly, the "cost-saving devices" handy to these employers are retrenchment, cut in wages and cancellation of negotiated benefits among other anti-labour measures. Government as employer of labour is also guilty of these unjust measures often informed by the rule of the thumb. Labour, at all levels of analyses accounts for less than 10 per cent of cost. Thus, the spectre of "cost-saving devices" must turn elsewhere; prohibitive interest rates, bloated executive pay, corporate fraud and endless examples of profound mismanagement.

The message here is: if we do not halt the unjust measures that shift the burden of the economic crisis on labour and labour alone, we should expect less in terms of productivity. This is because productivity itself is a means to an end: good life. We should therefore work towards the creation of that irreducible minimum level of comfort for all those expected to produce so that they can produce more. World Development Report of 1995 shows that the singular factor in higher productivity and economic growth in East Asian economies is heavy investment in physical and human capital, with special emphasis on human resources. This is one example in productivity scheme worthy of emulating in Nigeria.

What about the Unionists?*

Alhaji Uba Ahmed, the Honourable Labour and Productivity Minister, recently told the News Agency of Nigeria (NAN) that the detained scribe of Union of Petroleum and Gas Workers (NUPENG) Chief Frank Kokori is not a trade unionist but "…only a union employee". Agency report quoted the minister as saying that the employee status of Kokori in the union denied him his plea.

The clemency plea for the other four, the minister said, to be unionists (as distinct from union employees) explained why they were set free. Since the Minister's disclosure, this reporter has moved into action, if only to ascertain the actual role of ministers in the release of detainees.

My random survey reveals some divided and controversial opinions on the Minister's claims. Why some agree that ministerial input could matter on state security, there are others who seriously disputed the impression created by Alhaji Uba Ahmed that ministerial plea automatically translates into clemency. Some are pettily mischievous; arguing that judging from their vehemence and unrepentant posturing, the said released detainees never sounded like people that were in any way pleaded for. Definitely not in the least by a minister whose ground for a plea must have been conditional on 'good' behaviour and guided utterances they insisted. Observers said given the fact that freed detainees are as recalcitrant as NUPENG president, it is doubtful if the minister would risk his honour for detainees, who on release would call the bluff of the government. Some extremist views are even less benign; they suggested ministerial blackmail of the presidency noting that a sensitive issue such as

---

* April 1996

detention is exclusively a presidential business and not any ministry's burden. Their evidence is that the released unionists were detained well before the appointment of the Honourable Minister for reasons well articulated by the Head of State himself (not the then minister of Labour) indicating that detention is an extra-ministerial affair. They therefore maintained that the detention and release of the persons is not a labour issue as the minister would want us to believe. It is said to be a political/state affair, the credit or discredit of which needs not be attributed to a ministerial plea or lack of it. At best the public is urged to see the recent release of four unionists as part of commendable reconciliatory gesture already extended to other detainees by the Head of State, General Sani Abacha. Whatever the discordant views on Alhaji Uba's controversial claims on detainees are, we must revisit the subject of union membership which he vaguely touched on when he asserted that Kokori is only a union employee and not a unionist. Who actually are the trade unionists? What about them? A trade union is a voluntary organization of workers formed for the purpose of improving their terms and conditions of work. The definition states only the obvious. It is hardly illuminating in understanding the complex reality of the trade union movement. History and practices of unions in different work-places and countries actually define the character and objectives of the unions. For instance in Nigeria, "workers" are classified into "junior" and "senior" workers with the former belonging to the industrial unions while the latter belong to associations. By law, some hybrid "workers", so-called "essential services" also workers exist who are prohibited from forming unions altogether. Prohibition offends the principle of voluntarism but this has been the practice in Nigeria since colonial times. Trade union purpose is also problematic. Will unions' responsibility end at work-place or extend to civil society and in what form? Debates abound on this question.

Whatever the character and orientation of the unions may be, what will not be disputed is the fact that unions must be founded on the principles of unity, independence and democratic methods. Secondly since trade unions are organizations whose activities cover national and even international industrial landscape, they must have some forms of government or administrative set up that will ensure

22

representation and delegation. The members of union government are either elected or appointed. In labour circles, the elected and appointed are referred to as part-time officers (PTOs) and full-time officers (FTOs) respectively. These categories of officers are the trade unionists. Trade unionists are the visible representatives or delegates of the union. They include shop-stewards, branch officers, zonal officers, elected and appointed national officers such as the Presidents and General Secretaries. To this extent, for anybody to hold that Monsieur Kokori, the General Secretary of NUPENG is not a unionist but "only a union employee" amounts to a deliberate petty confusion. All trade unionists are "employees" of the union whether they are "employed" on "part-time" or "full-time" basis whether they are "employed" through elections or appointment.

Nothing has been subject of much confusion and misunderstanding as the relationship between PTOs and FTOs in the union. It is unfortunate if this confusion now finds expression at the labour ministry. If allowed it is capable of misinforming trade union policy. Any attempt to erect a discredited Berlin-Wall between "part-time" and "full-time" officers will be untenable. This is because in reality, such division is nebulous if not academic. For instance, to what extent can we say the work of elected union officers released by their employers to do eight-hour union work is "part-time"?

Trade union work is inherently on full-time basis as representation and delegation in the world of work cannot be done piecemeal. Once workers "employ" you either through election or appointment, as long as the tenure lasts, it is on full-time. Representation is indivisible in trade union movement. The same perspective applies to the misplaced notion that FTOs are paid career officers and PTOs are not. All trade unionists are paid officers of the union in proportion to their level of contribution and work in the union. This is not to deny the point that differences of responsibilities exist between FTOs and PTOs. On the contrary, the point to emphasize here is that both the FTOs and PTOs are two sides of the same coin: the unionist.

The most contentious issue however is where sovereignty ultimately resides in the union; in elected or appointed office.

Appointment/Election issue is a recurrent theme in the trade union movement. It is time the issue was openly discussed. The unions are very well alive to this fact in daily administration. Indeed most union constitutions make it clear that elected officers preside over such organs as executive councils and working committees, which underscore their status in the union bureaucracy. The facts of election and payment of dues (check-off) confer some sovereign powers in elected officers. Although one should note that there are some unions whose "full-time" principal officers such as the General Secretaries are also elected and equally pay their dues.

One important point however is the fact that election is only an important but not exclusive source of union authority. The primary mandate of the union is to protect members' interest and alleviate deplorable working conditions. Thus the real power of the union lies in the organizational and negotiation skills as well as the knowledge to get results for the ordinary union member in a complex work environment. Elected officers know that appointed officers who can talk the management language and check management excesses wield equally, if not considerable more powers and that they actually represent the pillars upon which the unions rest. Indeed the PTOs know that FTOs are the organizers, negotiators, educators, i.e. the real unionists. The challenge of modern unionism has made unions accept that even when appointed officers come from outside, they are no more 'outsiders' but insiders.

In summary, any attempt to draw a line between unionists along part-time and full-time, elected or appointed divide is artificial. As the democratization of the dissolved unions and NLC gathers momentum, trade union policy must foster comradeship and solidarity between unionists and not invent imaginary division. One policy option could be that all appointed officers, who in any case work and think for unions on full-time basis, must also pay their check-off. Principal full-time office holders such as General Secretary should also prepare to face election to avoid sit-tight syndrome and ensure members' confidence. Conversely, nothing as such stops elected officers from becoming full-time officers either, given that their experiences will be useful to the members. This is already happening. The present generation of FTOs were also PTOs (before 1978 restructuring of unions). In the main, they all grew from the industry. Let this experience in rich fusion and border-crossing, so to say, continue. The Imoudus, Kaltungos and Jalingos were once PTOs before they became FTOs, i.e. 'union employees'. This in no way denies them the status of trade unionists, which of course they are. The lesson of union's experiment in organization for the civil society is that nothing is inherently sacrosanct about appointed and elective offices. The issue is the extent the aspirations of members are met. I think once no one combines the rather difficult responsibilities of both the PTOs and FTOs simultaneously, oligarchic tendencies will be checked while unions will be truly democratic, all hopefully to the benefit of the rank and file.

On the whole, the point cannot be over-emphasized that all "employees" of unions whether appointed or elected are trade unionists. There may very well be "bad" or "good" unionists but unionists they are nonetheless. Let objective facts not become a subject of petty politics and unnecessary subterfuge.

Restoring Trade Union Independence*

Today is May Day. Yet just like the previous year and even the year before, there will be no celebration. Trade Unions are in despair. The greatest challenge lies in how to restore hope to the ranks of the labour movement. One evidence of the crises facing labour was recently dramatized by the reported frantic efforts of the former president of the Nigeria Labour Congress (NLC), Alhaji Ali Chiroma, to assume office as the sole administrator of National Union of Petroleum and Gas Workers (NUPENG). It will be recalled that Comrade Chiroma was himself a victim of dissolution when the Ibrahim Babangida administration ordered the police occupation of the Congress secretariat in 1988.

It is indeed paradoxical that Comrade Chiroma is "profiting" from dissolution through a belated appointment as a sole administrator of an affiliate union of the Congress. As a former faithful servant of the former NLC president, this writer felt saddened that any unionist of note would be presiding over any union either by default or through ministerial conspiracy as it is being alleged in the case of Chiroma's appointment. This development underscores the problems and challenges confronting the trade unions.

Let the point be made; trade unions face a risk of total collapse as comrades make a desperate move to run the unions through the back-door. The point cannot be over emphasized that one of the cherished principles of unionism is independence. By independence, it means that the unions should not be controlled either by the government, employers, political parties, fraternal international

---

* *Vanguard*, 1st May 1996, pg 7

organisations or 'veteran' unionists. Unions must be run and controlled only by their members. Perhaps there may be rare instances when the government or any external force may want to intervene in the affairs of some unions, which fail to manage their own affairs responsibly. Even in those instances, whoever intervenes must serve as a facilitator to return the unions to the path of independence and accountability. The fact that the NLC and some unions are still under the heels of government-appointed administrators during this year's May Day, contrary to earlier promises, shows that the current intervention is proving an exception to the rule.

What even makes the intervention suspect is the desperate attempt by the government functionaries to re-invent the unions. Even when it is out fashion, these functionaries are acting Mungo Park's 'rediscovering' River Niger as if the people who lived by the river never knew it was there in the first instance. Decree No. 4 of 1996 chooses to 'reinvent' the country's trade unions by providing legal backing for the restructuring of the hitherto 41 into 29 industrial unions as well as redefining union membership through exclusion of "non-card-carrying members". These two aspects of the decree, namely, the restructuring of unions and redefinition of union membership, are now subject of intense controversy in the labour cycles.

There is a general consensus that the decree lacks the benefit of necessary quality control which relevant labour agencies such as the Labour Advisory Council (LAC) could offer on such an important legal instrument. Indeed the tripartite labour advisory council made up of employers, ministry officials and labour unions was never consulted on the decree.

What with the factual and historical inaccuracies in its preamble. Dates were not only mixed up but drafters did not get right the numbers of restructured unions in a decree with such national and international significance. The former adviser to the Minister of Labour, Salisu Mohammed, had to resign in protest, describing the decree as 'mediocre' and even alleged a calculated move to deliberately mislead the Head of State into signing it.

The Honourable Minister of Labour and Productivity, Senator Uba Ahmed, had admitted the scandalous errors in the decree. He, however, still insisted that in substance the new decree had some merits, alluding to its provisions which ostensibly 'returned' the unions to its 'true owners' namely "card-carrying-members". Yet it is the projected strength of this decree as favoured by the minister that actually represents its weakness perhaps even more than the scandalous errors and inaccuracies that are admittedly associated with it. The issue is that the ideas contained in the decree are 'ill-informed'.

Take the issue of union membership, for instance. People wondered if the ownership of trade unions had ever been in dispute such that a decree is not needed in the first instance to provide the basis for adjudication on it. When the Head of State, General Sani Abacha announced the dissolution of the executive councils of the NLC and some unions in 1994, it was clearly on account of "politically motivated" activities rather than any crisis about ownership of the unions. Indeed, it has been rightly argued that if there was any dispute at all on who owns the union, that dispute arose only as a logical outcome of the government's intervention in the affairs of labour. Such dispute is even further aggravated when those appointed to run unions in the interim now promote similar "politically motivated" activities such as redefining membership and determining who are eligible to hold union offices. It is self-evident that sole administrators are not share-holders in workers' organisations and that they needed not set rules for unionists.

Not even the most "comradely" of the government-appointed sole administrators would claim to be owners of the union or "card-carrying" members such that they could conveniently set agenda for the unions. The government is sufficiently well-informed about this. This explained why no dissolution decree authorizes any administrator to determine who union members are. This also explains why the government has repeatedly urged for the speedy exit of the administrators through immediate reconstitution of the dissolved unions.

The move by some administrators of unions to sit tight through contrived long-drawn but crisis-prone programmes certainly run counter to the spirit of the government intervention. As the workers mark May Day, it is clear that if there is any dispute about the ownership of unions at all it is certainly between usurpers (read: sole administrators) and not between unionists and unionists. The challenge before all today is how to urgently restore trade union independence.

The End of Work (I)[*]

Ordinarily, a positive relationship exists between economic growth and job creation. According to Chief Anthony Ani, the finance minister, overall economic performance in 1997 was not as bad if not good enough. Budget details have it that, though short of anticipated rate of 5.5% GDP grew by 3.77%, a marked improvement from the rate of 2.2% in 1995. Sectorial details were no less salutary; oil and agriculture sectors grew by 8.35% and 4.10% respectively. Fiscal operations recorded improvement given that internally generated revenue and external reserves substantially increased. All these, more than anything else, make the reported proposed retrenchment of 150,000 public employees inexplicable. Indeed positive economic indicators last year make mass recruitment (not mass retrenchment) logical, tenable and fair. This is what received wisdom teaches; economic growth must translate to expanded employment and prosperity for the citizens. Or are we saying ours is a "jobless growth?" If so, how desirable is growth without jobs in a developing economy as ours?

The official explanation has been that the recent rationalization is long over-due. We have been told umpteenth times that civil service is "over-staff" or "over-bloated" and that the country needs a 'trimmed' and 'efficient' civil service. Mass-retrenchment is said to be one pre-condition for the emergence of 'professional' and 'well motivated' civil service. This is precisely where the problem lies. How valid is it that a country of 103 million people is "overstaffed" with 500,000 civil servants?

[*] *New Nigeria* newspapers, Monday 2nd March, 1998, pg. 5

Market reformers and their institutional promoters such as the World Bank had long sold a miserable good-for-nothing image of public employment in sub-Saharan Africa. The market-place cliché is familiar; "over-staffed, under-paid and unproductive public sector". The peripatetic picture is seemingly clearly enough such that no data or explanation is offered. The policy implication is also self-evident; mass lay-offs. It is a sad commentary that this flawed assumption and its suspect policy-hang-over are finding expression in our labour market policy. The recent directive on staff rationalization reportedly issued from the office of the Secretary to the Federation underscores how unwittingly our labour market policy is over-burdened by received wisdom which tends to promise despair than hope. The indiscriminate application of sack directive to all agencies regardless of their constitutions betrays the belated advice that the rationalization be devoid of witch-hunting or victimization." How will a newly established public eye centre or yet to be commissioned psychiatric hospital with no record of employees' 'foul language' among other over-loaded criteria, reduce its workforce by 30 per cent without recourse to wizard-cum-witch-hunting and sheer workplace repression? Does this directive not undermine recent civil service reforms aimed at ensuring job security in the public sector? Public sector resource managers need not apply the crude cost assumptions already long jettisoned by some private sector operators. To some accountants and even economists with profit and loss orientation, there is no doubt that mass employment is costly particularly in relatively 'low-productivity' sector as ministries or parastatals, where value-added falls below pay. But mass unemployment and huge idle human capacity is even more expensive to the society both in the short and long terms. We may save on salaries of retrenched teachers, nurses and doctors and the police but society remains permanently hunted by the cost of such savings to public education, public health and public security respectively. There are costs, there are COSTS. The choice is certainly ours. But we must for once have a critical look at the meanings of 'size', 'efficiency' and 'value' within the context of public service and public good.

This administration has just commendably fashioned out a vision, expectedly to transform the political and social-economic sphere of Nigeria by the turn of the twenty-first century. The challenges Vision 2020 pose are enormous. The point must however be made that translating these challenges to reality rests on sound labour market policies. The implementation of those myriad of policy options contained in Vision 2010 Report depends on the quality as well as quantity of public personnel.

Nigeria must reaffirm its commitment to full employment. There are many jobs to be done, namely provision of water, health services, housing, poverty alleviation, information, education, tax-collection and good governance. All these beg for more and more hands. Full employment as a policy objective does not in any way mean there can be no employments restructuring arising as a result of say, deskilling or outright declining productivity. But this "frictional" unemployment only calls for greater challenges in the areas of training and retraining to over-come skill imbalances for instance, and not mass-lay-offs. The issue is that while crude oil or solid minerals are non-renewable resources, with appropriate policy-mix, labour is inexhaustibly renewable. Throwaway labour-force represents potential output denied to the economy, its value-crudely subtracted – not added.

But before we proclaim the end of work for such a large number of civil servants as reportedly being proposed, we should consider the plight of those involved. Perhaps we may for once consider the plight of that person suddenly and arbitrarily retrenched. If he or she is the breadwinner, it is clear then that the family support collapses. Food may be difficult to get to feed the children with all the implications for malnutrition. Some kids may be withdrawn from school on account of non-payment of school fees while Easter and Sallah cloth will necessarily elude them. Pray the family is not sick either. Since the breadwinner cannot meet expectation, depression logically replaces love within the household. The options before retrenched men and women in a society without social security like Nigeria are therefore better imagined. The point is that in Nigeria, official hesitation must precede mass termination. May the knowledge and appreciation of the dire economic consequences of joblessness temper the outcome of the recent sack directive. It's time we opted for kinder and humane road to growth and development. Labour market policies with human-face will definitely prove an acid-test in this direction.

Wage Crisis: a Nigerian Paradox[*]

For better, for worse, minimum wage crisis has thrown up a number of paradoxes that must interest students and practitioners of industrial relations in particular and social and development issues in general. The first of such paradoxes lies in its timing. Memory is increasingly out of fashion in Nigeria. But we can only do without history at our peril. Early this century, the first generation of Nigerian workers, namely non-unionised civil servants, railway men and teachers sought for fairness at work. The outcry of the workers against the predatory colonial employers was instructively over poor remuneration. History does repeat self, but hardly in the same uncaring form as in Nigeria. It is ironic that Nigerian workers would enter the twenty-first century and indeed the new millennium again with the battle cry for adequate return on work. What must have then happened to growth and development and the expected trickle-down benefits the citizens were promised at Independence?

The responses of the colonial employers to the demands of the first generation workers for adequate pay took the forms of reluctance, racist arrogance, threat of mass sack, subterfuge of varying dimensions and in many instances, sheer brutality. Today's responses as vividly displayed during the last days of the former military administrators ironically are also true to colonial legacies. Witness, for instance, how departing military administrators competed among selves to short-change their own employees, with methods ranging from smear campaign that workers would 'truncate the transition' to direct threat of (and actual job-losses) and not in few instances, state violence against strikers. The gang of military

[*] *The Guardian*, Wednesday 30th June, 1999, pg 49

administrators of so-called nineteen northern states actually met to pay their work-force less than national average, as a mark of their curious contribution to even national development.

With civil rule, the minimum wage crisis is certainly far from being over. What is however instructive is the fact that workers' just struggle has outlived the unjust military administrators who paradoxically fell casualties of their own prophecy of job losses. Thanks to the new wind of change that has retrenched those whose ground for negotiation with their workers is retrenchment blackmail.

Another discernible irony in the wage crisis lies in the news that thirty-six newly inaugurated State governors plan to define a common position on the minimum wage crisis. It seems, what party partisanship ordinarily would not make possible, minimum wage crisis is feverishly bringing in unison. Which in turn underscores the all-inclusive nature of labour and socially related issues? A lowly paid worker is a hungry worker and his anger will be the same irrespective of party affiliation. This is one common sense that eluded military administrators but which is happily, now common among our politicians. Yet, as good as this new civil approach of the new civilian administrators to the minimum wage crisis, the relevance of its outcome still rests on their perspective of the intractable compensation crisis Nigeria found itself. Sadly, politicians' views about the wage issue are far from being different from that of their discredited military counterparts.

Most commentators had tried to devalue workers' claim to decent earnings in the typical old fashion. Workers, we are told constitute an 'insignificant number', representing 'only 5' or 'only 10%' of the population (depending on the preferred rate of workers' devaluation). Whatever are the merits or demerits of these claims, what will not be disputed is the fact that the naughty issue of minimum wage which ostensibly affects an 'insignificant' section of the population had kept all of us restless. Somebody must certainly unravel the riddle that makes minimum pay meant for an assumed minimum number of the populace, generate such a maximum discomfort for all. This means there must certainly be more than the commentators would want us to believe.

The wage crisis, more than anything else, is a true test of what we choose to make out of our new democratic dispensation. It is commendable that the Ad hoc Committee on teachers' crisis set up by the House of Representatives accorded teachers' plight the necessary attention by making a case for the resolution of the pay crisis. That it was a refreshing reminder of superiority of representation and delegation over studied indifference and criminal cynicism of the past military dictatorship. It is also on record that the Lower House had demonstrated greater sensitivity to people's plight than the Senate. The eventual disbursement of fund by Obasanjo's presidency to pay the teachers indicates the fact that if there is the will to resolve the wage crisis, there will always be the ways and the means.

The greatest paradox of the wage crisis however lies in the reality that those who are most vehement in laying claim to championing the cause of the oppressed are the most vicious in undermining workers' legitimate struggle for decent earnings. Much had been reported about Archbishop Okogie\NLC face-off on the minimum wage. Observers are surprised that a priest would so viciously and consistently berate teachers who ordinarily deserve our sympathy and support in their demand for improved teaching standard. However if Okogie's is another distinctively Nigerian paradox (that those who should help the weak scorn them) what about the comments by former NLC president, Paschal Bafyau, that the minimum wage rates are "unrealistic". This 'labour-on-labour' unusual paradox understandably has provoked more controversy. Some choose to see Paschal's anti-workers' new mission as being consistent with his controversial past record of inconsistency, double-talk and sheer betrayal in the labour movement. They contrast Paschal's slippery tenure as labour leader with those of tested, steadfast, consistent and respected unionists such as Pa Imoudu and Alhaji Hassan Sunmonu who have been unambiguous in their support for the current move of NLC to restore the lost glory of Nigerian working class particularly under Pascal's leadership. Others are even less benign with the former NLC leader, seeing Pascal Bafyau's comment as attention-drawing strategy of a comrade-turned-failed politician. They however maintain that since he is neither an elected senator nor elected representative nor even ministerial nominee, his views on wage determination are inconsequential and thus be ignored. Whatever is the correct assessment of Pascal's position should be left to history. But the views of AD chieftain and ministerial nominee, Chief Bola Ige, certainly matters, since they impact considerably on the pattern of resources-allocation in the states under the heel of Alliance for Democracy. For instance, Osun State governor, Chief Akande had repeated Chief Ige's argument that because AD's States would implement the much trumpeted free education and free health, they need not pay the same wage as their predecessors. Indeed Osun State, had reportedly cut the minimum wage to ₦1,300.00 thus having the dubious record of being the first State to return us to strikes commendably suspended by NLC on the eve of new democratic dispensation.

The Berlin Wall, Chief Bola Ige wanted to erect between decent pay and free education and health passes for another Nigerian paradox. Ordinarily the issues the respected politician wants to pitch against each other are not mutually exclusive. Indeed one cannot do without the other. Those who will teach free education must live on decent pay and not slave wages, otherwise they will offer miserable slave instructions and not free citizens' education. Conversely, for the scores of thousands of Nigerian medical workers to return from Saudi Arabia or South Africa or wherever they are offering free health to other citizens, the pay offer at home must be attractive enough. The most recent memory does not support Ige's fallacy either. He had repeatedly inundated us that Awolowo is his eternal mentor. Awolowo offered free education and health and even more minimum wage than the NPN government that never laid claim to welfare policies at all. Given Awolowo's belief in living (and not necessary minimum wage), it was actually the UPN's insistence on 300 naira that made NPN government to quickly settle for 120 naira minimum wage following the historic NLC strikes in 1981.

The wage crisis presents the real acid test for our new democrats. It must reveal to us the difference between democratic lip-service and democratic actions by democratic actors.

Labour and Development[*]

Will labour prove Abdulsalami Abubakar's 'acid test'? Head of state's 'acid test' lies in his repeated affirmative commitment to democratize the country's polity and society. Labour's variant of this 'test' can be found in July 20th maiden broadcast, which serves the notice of unions' democratisation during the 'life of this administration'. Other 'testy' steps include eventual release of detained unionists, namely Frank Kokori and Milton Dabibi, the repeal of dissolution decrees 9, 10 and 24 (as they related to NLC, NUPENG, PENGASSAN, ASUU and NASU almost in that order) and the recent handing over of the Congress' administration to a committee of labour unionists.

Labour's democratisation assumes special importance given that recent Nigeria's history shows that what happens to labour is the true measure of any promise about transition to civil and democratic rule by the military. We can only be indifferent to events in labour at even greater expense to the nation's transition programme to democracy. Not only because labour remains the most important factor in civil society, but precisely because trade unions have become veritable guinea pigs with which the military put to test its designs, (for better, for worse), before imposing them on the larger society as a whole. On can almost establish one-to-one relationship between the country's labour practice and the national social and political behaviour and say that when the former is bad as it is usually, the latter ultimately would be disastrous.

When in 1988, Chiroma-led NLC executive was abruptly dissolved under the self-serving official argument of preventing ideological rivalry in a non-governmental organisation, nobody

---

[*] 1999

38

realised that it was a dress-rehearsal for greater future violations and rape of national rights by a budding dictatorship. The lesson therein is clear, albeit late and painful; that when the mandate of well over two million workforce that the Congress represented was forcefully denied without a blinker (and even with some curious justification by those who should know better), unwittingly, we had laid the ground for subsequent cynical assault on fourteen million national mandate. The event of 1993 was certainly a logical outcome of series of injustices experimented and tested out from day one in the labour movement by an authoritarian regime.

Take the notoriously recurring factor of sole-administrator), being today's regular trademark of military's management practices. No other sector of the society has got such a disproportionate share of government -imposed sole administrators as the labour movement. Spanning two decades (from Murtala\Obasanjo era to Abacha regime), unions have been turned into some laboratories whereby some obsolete management (or is it mismanagement?) practices are carried out. Indeed it will not be out of place to say that 'success' of sole administratorship (read: sole dictatorship) in labour movement explains why it is today also being indiscriminately applied to parastatals, local and state governments and even universities with all the attendant 'successes' recorded in these organisations. All the above explain why we should not be indifferent to what happens to labour as its fallout ultimately hunts the nation. Hence the timely relevance of the question, "will labour prove another military's acid test on democratisation?" Or better still, how do we assist labour to democratize as a necessary step towards successful democratisation of the larger society?

Answers to these questions are as complicated as the terrain that is labour. But one issue is self-evident: success or otherwise of labour's transition process largely depends on the sincerity and commitment of the federal government and its relevant agencies. This is because democratisation of labour becomes an issue today precisely as a result of government undemocratic intervention in labour uncalled for in the first instance. It is therefore gratifying that, steps taken so far by the government point to some progress in the direction of the much needed official disinterestedness. Government disinterestedness is one necessary condition for genuine labour's democratisation. The extent to which Abacha's octopus spread pillaging and rampaging tentacles to the juicy sectors of the economy had understandably dominated the media. Bigger pictures of atrocities loom large in mind. This however does make the smaller variants of tyranny less important more so that it was the unreported success in micro-crimes that encouraged the criminals to hold the nation a hostage.

The bane of Abacha regime's labour policy (which in reality is labour *policing*) lies in unimaginable meddlesomeness. The official involvement in the affairs of non- governmental organisations takes the forms of divisive legislation that promoted exclusion of independent and enlightened unionists, deliberate tactics of divide and conquer, criminalization of normal union civil functions, emergency of new crisis merchants (read; security officials) claiming sole ability to tame labour and introduction of non-union methods of thuggery and violence.

This is why the speeches and actions of the new Honourable Minister of Labour and Productivity certainly reveal a welcome departure from the authoritarian and partisan conduct and utterances of his predecessor. Dr Emmanuel Udogu's insistence on all- inclusive labour's process, non-hijacking of labour's electoral process, non-funding of unions and non-promotion of divisive tactics is instructive. For once, it confirms the fact that in the recent past, labour's playing field was deliberately littered with landmines with the main objective of crippling the movement. Abacha's perverse politics of exclusion, legislation-overload with unprecedented outer-clauses, disregard of international standard willingly subscribed to by the country, subversive funding of political process to serve self-succession agenda, cronyism of the worse bent, lootacracy and criminalization of civil society through phony security claims were initially tested out in trade unions. Which again supports the view that labour offers an insight to what could happen to the larger society? Thus when the secretary of the 13-man committee presently overseeing the Congress' affairs Comrade Adebayo Kazeem was only saying the obvious that labour never had it so bad with a bad minister under a worse regime. What with the ways the unions which are open organisations were held in worse suspect, manifesting in incitement of police against workers' meetings, malicious prosecution of seminar worker- participants, prohibitive decrees that set unionists against unionists and grossly violated the ratified ILO conventions, vandalization of unions' properties under government- appointed administrators and government funding of non-unionists to undermine union independence. Thus whether labour will conclusively prove the test of democratisation or not depends above all on the willingness and the speed with which the government sets to hand off labour, which in the first instance is not its business.

Hope for democratized labour therefore does not lie in wishful (or rather mischievous) thinking of 'no administrator in the next 100 years' as expressed by the ex-NLC administrator, Ahmed Gusau. On the contrary, once government concentrates on the all-engaging business of governance and allow unionists and (not 'comrade' administrators, it imposes) to run the unions, definitely unions will remain independent until eternity. This is why it is necessary that the present Honourable Minister is encouraged to continue the good work of government disengagement by pushing for the repealing the remaining vestiges of meddlesomeness which decrees 4, 26 and 29 particularly stand for and scores of other obnoxious laws that impose undue rigidities in the labour market. Everybody stands to gain when government (read: military) settles down to do its statutory functions.

But government disinterestedness only resolves half of the riddle, Abubakar's 'acid test' throws up for the labour movement. The other half-riddle tests the preparedness of unionists for the challenge of democratisation. So far unions' actions support the views that unionists are eager to get the government off the back of labour. The relative ease with which the naughty issue of unexpired 'mandate' of the old executives of the Congress was addressed represents a lesson in positive-sum nature of power bargaining in a society recently weakened by 'mandate\no-mandate' - zero-sum politics. The all-inclusive constitution of the caretaker committee by unionists themselves also put paid to the divide and rule objectives of decrees 4 and 26, thus making their official abrogation an urgent

41

formality. All this, above all, serve appropriate notice that civil society can organise self once government demonstrates good fate and does no lurk around the corner to promote disunity. As labour drama unfolds, the challenge lies in how to ensure credible labour's transition process with the ball in unionists' court. This explains why labour observers were surprised that some 'unionists' sought court injunctions to halt the long awaited process.

Obasanjo: Labour Dimension*

Now that subjective and partisan assessment of the Obasanjo administration fills the air, an objective assessment lies in a critical look at its record on labour issues. Interestingly, today is May-Day, third in the new democratic beginning. Third time the Special Guest of Honour (or is it a Special Comrade?) at May-Day parade, President Olusegun Obasanjo eminently qualifies as labour's friend assuming honouring May-Day invitations equals friendship.

Eternal credit still goes to PRP government of Balarabe/Rimi and Shehu Shagari NPN-led government (in that order) for making workers' day work-free in 1981, at a time it was unpopular to do so. Chief Obasanjo, however, remains the only President of the Republic that has kept faith with workers' day three times (if he honours this year's) with a face-cap taking workers' salute on a May-Day. He actually flew in from Burkina Faso to attend last year's May-Day which earned him the NLC title of a 'Chief Worker'. No thanks to the recent past, when labour issues were criminalized and labour-day was officially scorned. Even today, few state Governors are 'May-Day compliant', notable ones being Kaduna's Makarfi and Lagos' Tinubu, making the President's consistent gesture more than symbolic. May-Day under OBJs refutes the current cheap blackmail in town that this dispensation is synonymous with Abacha's dictatorship. It is *not* and could not have been anyway. The difference is clear between 'nascent' democracy and ancient dictatorship.

Chief Obasanjo is not new to labour terrain. He concluded the controversial labour reform, initiated by General Murtala in 1976.

* *The Guardian*, May 1st, 2002, pg. 45

43

That reform led to the current single labour centre (more for official easy control than preferred value of workers' unity), automatic check-off and industrial unionism. He was also the first presidential candidate to attend the first ever workers' parley for presidential hopefuls in 1999, belatedly followed by Chief Olu Falae, AD, sorry, APP candidate. In that interactive session, following Oshiomhole's insistence and articulation of workers' expectations, candidate Obasanjo laid bare his programmes for national development, some of which included commitment to democratic values, improved earnings, employment generation, industrialisation, poverty eradication as well as consultation and workers' participation on issues of development. The question today is: to what extent has the President lived up to his promises?

By and large, freedom of association and assembly is respected by this administration. Thanks to the NLC under the leadership of Oshiomhole, that lived up to its new beginning campaign; willing and able to legitimately take the advantage of new democratic space to advance the workers' interests. Obasanjo's successive appearances at May-Day legitimise this singularly cherished right, given that May-Day is nothing but workers' exercising their freedom as contained in the 1999 constitution and relevant ILO conventions Nos 87 and 98. Significantly too, the last three years witnessed robust contestation and cooperation between labour and government. NLC rightly turned out workers and general public demanding moderation of the part of the then indulgent legislators, more preoccupied with allowances, rather than law-making. No doubt, allowances still constitute a source of acrimony in the Assembly no less than they are in Anambra state. But the increasing qualitative legislative activism we now witness is largely attributable to labour's earlier push. The Congress more than once engaged the Federal and State executives on policy issues of deregulation of the oil sector (read: fuel price increase) and minimum wage agreements. CBN was not spared, as NLC rightly bemoaned its seeming timidity as a regulatory and supervisory agency in the face of increasing unaccountability and impunity of bankers that has negatively impacted on interest rates and exchange rate of naira.

Labour and Development II*

NLC proved an exception to the increasing discordant (national) rule last week, when it hosted an international conference on development. The conference on 'Globalization and NEPAD; the role of the Trade Union Movement' was a joint effort between the Congress and International Confederation of Free Trade Unions – Africa Regional Organisation (ICFTU-AFRO). In view of the fact that conflicts and political tensions nowadays boringly hit the headlines, NLC's initiative assumes a special importance. Refreshingly remarkable are the new insights thrown-up at this conference on familiar buzz words (or are they dogmas?) namely Globalization, NEPAD, Poverty Reduction Strategy Paper (PRSP), Privatisation, Equity, Gender, etc.

It became self-evident at this historic conference that defining these scores of development paradigms could hardly tame them. These concepts must therefore be put in critical historic and contemporary perspective. And precisely that was what the conference did. ILO resident representative's address lived up to this expectation. He gave the conference a unique gift by providing Fidel Castro's perspective on globalization as articulated during a South/South conference in Havana. Fidel's description departs from standard textbook definition, no less than it reflects the reality of globalization given the rounds of applause that greeted this informed perspective. Fidel aptly likened globalization to modern-day slave-expedition ship on the high sea with passengers of scandalous unequal means and access. While few crew members, mainly the slave masters who are also the captains, have access to all the

* *Daily Trust*, Monday 23rd September, 2002, pg. 6

comfort, inclusive of computers and mobile phones, a whole lot are in want of basic means of livelihood, inclusive of food, water and light. According to Fidel, the weight of injustices in this ship is capable of sinking it to the peril of all. Despair statistics by UN agencies about unequal distribution of world resources between the North (Europe and America in particular G-8) and the South (Asia, Africa and Latin America) a kind of global Apartheid as it were, and the attendant restlessness of the deprived makes Fidel's insight prophetic. There was almost a conclusion at this conference, that it has been 'their world (i.e. Europe and America) while 'we' (Africa) are onlookers, but for the profound problematic such conclusion poses for international working class solidarity and actions.

One remarkable strongpoint of this confab was the recurring historic perspective. Africa is so much in a hurry for development such that it has little time for reflection on where it was coming from. The result has been a vicious cycle of motions without a decisive qualitative movement. This conference is rich in history, an indispensable subject increasingly out of fashion in our school curriculum. We were told how today's developed economics were totally insular during their early take off contrary to the textbook notion of open societies. In some extreme cases as Japan and China, they were actually closed economies. America after independence rejected the theory of comparative advantage, which could have consigned it to agriculture as distinct from industry. America has since moved on to space. Today we uncritically take trade liberalization as an article of faith, told to scrap steel industry on account of 'inefficiency', an advice that South Korea rightly rejected in the 1960s. Hooked on policy advice on comparative advantage (which nobody has ever heeded), Africans are permanently made to be producers of primary goods and consumers of finished goods.

Still on history, the conference shows how present regional and continental efforts at integration (AU) are part of Africa's heritage as distinct from the current impression that it is another fad modelled after EU. Artificial borders and restrictions are mere colonial inventions. How these historic insights would inform the continent's present policy choices, is the challenge for policy makers. What is however clear that, integration is far from being appreciated beyond

46

lip service. While ECOWAS has for instance, recorded some progress at integration (more so with labour mobility), the absence of a common currency shows that financial integration is still a tall order. In respective African countries, Chinese walls are being erected to undermine internal integration. In Nigeria, for instance, bastardization of States and local governments creation, driven primarily by politics of distribution rather than economics of production have reopened old village boundaries and hatreds that in turn undermine internal integration. The issue is that there cannot be regional integration when we are faced with prospects of internal disintegration.

On NEPAD, there was consensus that this development paradigm represents some commendable departure from the past. That African leaders now wish to relate with the world leaders as 'partners' and not as subordinates was novel, if not revolutionary. But the content of this partnership was the subject of intense debate. Will the relations be dependent, independent or interdependent? So far, NEPAD's notion of partnership is seemingly dependent, with expectation of billion dollars financial flows from the G-8. Debt cancellation will freeze twice as much as the expected resources for the continent. Yet NEPAD is debt-cancellation shy, it prefers debt relief. Charity must begin at home. African leaders are expected to first build partnership with their own citizens before cultivating partnership with 'outsiders'. To this extent, NEPAD was berated for its top-down orientation with the conference insisting that the document can still benefit more with workers' inputs. The importance of social dialogue demands that NEPAD should be outcome of popular participation, at conceptual and implementation level. NEPAD sets clear growth rates targets, but its labour markets policy targets are not clear. What jobs will NEPAD's desired growth generate? Will it be jobless growth of the discredited SAP era? It is gratifying that the ILO is assisting to factor in the employment component of NEPAD. What then about the quality of expected investment and jobs? Will it be sustainable growth, with sustainable decent jobs? Or is it foreign investment without foreign funds (witness NITEL – ill-fated sales)? Or investment without respect for minimum labour standards including health and safety (witness Ikorodu West African rubber and plastic company tragedy)?

The role of international financial institutions, namely IMF and World Bank expectedly generated more passion. The IMF and World Bank are two sister institutions trade unions love to hate on account of their anti-labour policy advice. Very interesting that both are now on a roundtable with unions discussing the linkage between growth and poverty reduction, even if this round table discussion witnessed rounds of acrimonies. It is not yet the end of Cold War between the two great defenders of the Market (IMF and World Bank) and unapologetic defenders of the State (the unions). Yet some shift emerged from this conference even if it was all about change without changes.

For instance, IMF and World Bank now recognise the role of State and Unions in development, no more as obstacles to development. Now we hear of 'good' governance and programme ownership from institutions that long played ostrich with politics. Interestingly unions are increasingly coming to terms with the truism that they cannot be doctrinaire in condemning neo-liberal policies just because they are being pushed by IMF or World Bank. Take privatisation for instance, it was clear that the issue is not 'yes' or 'no' but to what extent do either public or privatized enterprises, promote and guarantee jobs, ensure delivery of services at affordable prices. Trade unions seem to accept that both the market and state are means and not the ends of development. The ends should be employment generation and public welfare.

The Poverty Reduction Strategy Paper (PRSP) was subjected to profound assessment. The intriguing question (or is it suspicion?) is; what is the business of IMF whose policy advice on devaluation, removal of subsidy promoted poverty between mid-1980s to early 90s, got to do with poverty reduction? The Fund is hunted with its recent unsavoury history in promoting misery, which in turn creates legitimacy crisis for PRSP. But there are those who argue rather cynically that there is no better institution that can eradicate poverty than the institution that promotes it in the first place. All that is needed is policy reversal. And that is precisely what the Fund is not willing to do.

Which explains why the conference resolves that the PRSP needs to be "comprehensively repackaged in a way that demonstrates commitment of western nations and the international finance institutions to Africa, especially in the areas of debt forgiveness, greater overseas development assistance and market access" The fundamental question however is that why should wealthy African countries like Nigeria for instance be discussing Poverty Reduction Paper, when its preoccupation should be wealth generation and wealth distribution?

Life after Work[*]

Today (Tuesday December 17, 2002) marks the climax of the campaign by NLC aimed at drawing attention to the ever-deteriorating plight of pensioners. Rallies were organised last week by the state councils of the Congress with similar goal of reminding those who still care that life after work in Nigeria is still regrettably miserable. It is quite remarkable that the state rallies once again exposed how uncaring Nigeria is with its own citizens who once helped to built it. This is one qualitative fact never captured in this year's UNDP country report of despair. Last Wednesday, thanks to NLC campaign, we knew that Cross River State government owes pensioners 20 months' pay totalling ₦1 billion. Ironically this is a state that just recently insensitively committed scarce resources to accursed Miss World Contest. Indeed, first lady of Cross River proudly announced donations of scores of mobile handsets to 90 "queens" for them to communicate with their relations at home during the contest that never held. In the same state, we now know that pensioners communicate with their 'mobile' placards which last Wednesday read: "Broken Homes Created by Irregular payment of Pension. Government should be sensitive to the plight of pensioners. Is it a crime to be a pensioner and is retirement a curse?"

In Anambra, in the last two years, 600 pensioners, according to NLC State council, died due to lack of money to fend for themselves. This figure is thrice the number of 200 that died in recent Kaduna mayhem, yet it went unreported until NLC pricked our conscience. Even the killer disease, AIDS would not kill 600 in 2 years as non-payment of pensioners' entitlements did. In Kwara State, your guess

---

[*] *Daily Trust*, Monday 17th December 2002, pg. 6

is as good as mine, Pensioners are reportedly routinely cheated. State NLC listed the woes of pensioners as follows:

- Non-settlement of 150% arrears of pension as from January 2001 to date; which means the state government is owing the pensioners 24 months as at December 2002.
- Non-settlement of 30 months arrears of pension.
- Non-implementation of adjustments of monthly pension allowance for 1995 retirees.
- Non-completion of the pension payable to the officers who retired between 1st September and 31st December 1998 which is supposed to be based on the salary structure prevalent at that time.
- Non-payment of gratuity to local government pensioners as from 1996 to date.
- Even in Zamfara, the pathetic plight of pensioners is true to type. In Imo State, the state government owes pensioners 3 months' pay with effort to pay only one month which amount to between ₦150 and ₦300 monthly.

If public retired employees are so much humiliated and invariably being turned into destitute, then the plights of retirees in the private sector, (heaven of exploitation) is better imagined.

We must therefore commend NLC under Adams Oshiomhole, for reminding us, (if only one day), that we are not only unjust to serving working men and women but we are inexplicably callous in our (mal) treatment of our grandparents and parents called pensioners. Paradoxically NLC campaign held on the care of National Merit Award, in which, some select retired (but not tired) few are collecting third 'national award', while unknown thousands of retirees are owed ten months pay. So much for our sense of fair-play!

Pensioners' lot represents the worst dimension of crisis of compensation, yours truly reflected upon last week. The truth is that ultimately every working man and woman must get fatigue one day. Whether we want it or not, senility must eventually replace today's abundant energy. Hence the need to prepare for the proverbial raining days by setting aside some funds that will at least meet the subsistence needs of the aged workers. The above constitute the principles that informed the establishment of pension in the public sector. These principles are still certainly valid today.

The issue of 'life after work' was far more important to be left to the wishes of private sector employers. Which then also explain, why as far back as 1961, through an Act of Parliament, the country's founding fathers, established National Provident Fund (NPF). Sadly, we have perverted the above historic concerns for retired employees through gross mismanagement, corruption and sheer diversion of pension funds especially in the public sector. It is gratifying however to see some remarkable innovations in the private sector's pension scheme. The transformation of NPF to National Social Insurance Trust Fund (NSITF) under the able management of its immediate past MD, Dr. Abba Aji and the current, Dr. Rufai Mohammed shows that if there is the will, there must be many ways to address the concerns of workers after work. It is to the credit of NSITF that retired contributors are reported collecting their pay as at when due, compared to public sector pensioners that are sent to their graves without their dependants collecting their entitlements.

But as significant as NSITF's efforts are, so long as public pensioners groan for their legitimate rights, a dark shadow is cast on the entire Nigeria social security system. With the collapse of the extended family support and traditional values of historic care and concern for the aged especially since the beginning of notorious structural adjustment, every active and young worker today can only ignore the issue of pension scheme at the instance of his/her sustenance after work. Pension schemes constitute an important and integral part of total compensation for workmen and women.

The truth of the matter is that pensioners are caught between the two extremes, namely official government neglect and public sympathy, none of which is beneficial to them. Pension is a legitimate right of workers. It is a deferred payment, which both the workers and employers must set aside so that workers at old age will not be living on some charity as if they are destitute. The challenge lies in how to make this principle work in Nigeria. The bane of public sector pension lies in its non-contributory character. The pension scheme is still regulated by obsolete Pensions Act of 1979 with all its amended provisions.

Precisely, because it is non-contributory, public servants are not required to contribute any financial sum into the schemes. Conversely it is assumed that somebody would devote some funds for the scheme which is increasingly not so. Civil servants automatically qualify for pension once they maintain some meritorious service and meet the required length of service, currently put minimum of ten years in the public service. Dismissed officers on account of grievous offences are however excluded. Until Public Pension Scheme is made to be contributory, it will be treated as no man's business depending on the whims and caprices of government officials. What makes NSITF relatively successful is its contributory character. Precisely because workers and employers do contribute, they are conscious of the need to manage the fund to the desired goal. Indeed the board of the Fund has workers' and employers' representatives unlike public sector pension scheme which is at discretion of Directors and Ministers who, in the first instance are eager to default on payment of current workers' salaries and see pensioners as ghost workers altogether.

The Minister of Defence, Lt. General Theophilus Danjuma, reportedly said ₦15 billion has been 'ear'marked (may not necessarily be 'hand' paid) for the pension of retired military personnel in next year's budget. While this constitutes some official sensitivity to the plight of pensioners, the questions are:

Is the sum enough to pay all entitlements? What is the source of this 'ear'marked sum? Have sums not been earmarked before? Were the pensioners paid? Is the sum currently provided for sustainable?

It is time the pension fund is reformed to make workers and government contribute for employees' life after work. Contributory scheme is clearly more sustainable. For one, it will be free from recurring government budget crisis (or is it budget confusion?). Secondly, workers and their unions will have more interest to manage the scheme they freely contribute into when they are at work rather than living it until they are out of work. The way we eventually resolve the existing pension crisis puts to test our real commitment to welfare of the citizenry, poverty eradication and even anti-corruption campaign. How much sermons a worker will listen to from the respected Akanbi Commission, when he/she knows that after work, nobody will listen to his/her outcries?

Labour and Democratic Process[*]

This year's workers' day assumes a special importance. Taking place against the background of a democratic transition, the critical question is; of what relevance is labour to Nigeria's democratic process? NLC seems conscious of the context of this year's workers' day, which explains its chose celebration theme: Consolidating Democracy.

Bjorn Beckman is one political economist that has done extensive original works on trade union performance in Nigeria. According to him, 'expressing dissent, organising alternative opinions, challenging those in power, and contesting for office are all central features of a democratic process'. His conclusion is that unions in Nigeria have passed democratic tests. In a country in which parties and party formations were once long prohibited by the military, only unions have been vehicles for democratic expression at work places and larger society. Unions held periodic elections, removed elected leaders and routinely re-elect new ones at a time it was unpopular to do so.

As recent as February this year, NLC organised its 8th Delegates' Conference. Nigeria marches on the road to the 4th Republic 42 years after independence. But NLC has inaugurated eight elected executive leadership in the past 25 years of its formation (NLC came into being in 1978). Congress' recent conference was adjudged as the most democratic in international labour movement. No party convention was as organised. Almost the whole day of the two-day conference was devoted to moving motions and counter motions by

[*] *Daily Trust*, Monday 5th May 2003, pg. 6

affiliate industrial unions on issues at work and society (job-creation and job retention, education and health, HIV, women participation, US-Iraq war, privatisation, etc.) Few hours were spent on elections of officers that were mostly unopposed. What was good for the NLC also proved same for its affiliate industrial unions. Just last week, Nigeria Union of Railway Workers (NURW) concluded its delegates' Conference. The union operates in a depressed sector; Railway workers are owned five months salaries while locomotives bought at whopping 12.6 billion naira from China under Abacha regime are not criminally functioning. Remarkable is that even under this depressed setting, NUR still held a free and fair elections. The lesson is that if contest for leadership is about service, there will always be contestation about how to get the job done, but consensus about who should do what will not be farfetched. This is the reverse at our national level in which the combat (not contest) is for the spoil of office. It is our pre-occupation with power and power without responsibilities, as it were, that is the bane of the polity.

NLC also recently conducted state council elections in all the 36 states and the Federal Capital. Not in one state was there a report of 'rigging' and discordant views that have since dominated the national politics since the recent series of elections. Again the lesson is that where power and power retention is about sacrifice, violence and acrimony must give way to enduring mutually rewarding outcomes.

One significant area labour has further advanced the cause of democracy, is active engagement of politicians to refocus them from mutually destructive preoccupation of politics of persons (and persons only) to mutually rewarding issue-centred politics. The NLC presidential parley remained the only pan-Nigerian, non-partisan forum attended by all notable presidential contenders. That forum brought the best, the ugly and the worse from all contestants, an expose that must have guided enlightened voters like workers to make enlightened choices. Also, NLC cultivated 4000 trained, experienced election monitors compared to 185 foreign observers (as if they were going to Mauritius).

Whatever the merits and demerits of international monitors and observers, their presence inadvertently reinforced the increasing self-doubt about our capacity to simply get going without some patronage. Energies we dissipate in endorsing and disputing the 'reports' of foreign observers (note; not participants) confirms the servile orientation of officialdom and the media alike. Why, should we catch cold, once, some observing (not participating) foreigners sneeze? Better still, why should the tail (which is everything foreign) wag the head (which everything local should be)?

International monitoring of electoral process is certainly not unimportant. It is even almost unavoidable, in a unipolar world in which, 'international best practices' are unilaterally imposed by Common Wealth (that we all know is far from being common) of European Union (that is not inclusive of a dark continent) and United States (that is disuniting the rest of the world). In any case, we could not have escaped being observed anyway. George Owen had long predicted that by the turn of the millennium, (Nineteen Eighty-Four) Big Brother would know what we do and don't do in our bedroom. In the age of satellite stations and CNN it is either you invite observers or they watch you anyway.

But for God's case, we must for once judge ourselves by our collectively defined standard rather than judging oneself from somebody 'prism'? We must reject the sickening patronizing view that we are 'nascent' in the conduct of free and fair elections and that some reports of so-called observers would mar and make our elections. Democratic conduct and traditions are part of our great heritage as we have seen with NLC experience. If we must 'observe' as we must, if we must 'monitor' as we must, our rich, albeit controversial (like anything democratic) history in democratic engagement should serve as reference point and not some externally defined prejudices and biases.

It is a scandal that a country with long dated democratic ideas of accountability and representation would kowtow to some sermons on 'good governance' by the very external forces that once shamelessly did business with dictatorships of varying colouration. It is a shame that we had to import ballot boxes from South Africa, a country, whose majority black citizenry could not be voted and be voted for on account of obnoxious system of apartheid at a time we were already vote-fatigued and vote-weary. Such is the level of degeneration and even loss of memory that we take the reports of international observers as article of faith.

Pension Act of 2004: Labour Dimension*

The issue is not to 'advocate labour's viewpoint' as such but to promote 'better conversation' about the Pension Act and the guidelines for its transitional arrangements. The idea is to lift us out of 'polarisation' of labour/employers/Pen COM divide and take us 'into a greater common sense'. The point is that what is good for labour may possibly not be bad for employers. Conversely what is good for employers and Pen COM may not be bad for the workers! Sustainable pension scheme should be a win-win scheme but that is ONLY if all stakeholders have open minds to accept as such and accordingly work towards the realisation of the scheme.

I found useful the diagnostic tool of SWOT analysis. It offers the framework to consider the Strengths (S), Weaknesses (W), Opportunities (O) and Threats of the Pension Act and the transitional guidelines in an objective way leaving room for possible policy measures and strategies for improvement. SWOT analysis is the middle tool between the two extremist tools of conflict model approach that sees nothing positive about the Act and the uncritical functionalist model that is averse to any criticism of the Act and the guidelines.

Strengths

Pension Act in principle represents a progressive labour legislation because it attempts to address the naughty issue of compensation after work.

---

* *Daily Trust*, Monday 5th December 2003, pg. 6

Pension Act legitimises a sustainable contributory scheme compared to the moribund non-contributory scheme. Section 1.2 of the guidelines reinforces this strength.

The scheme is also strong on corporate governance arrangements that are radically different from the past public sector schemes; National Pension Commission supervises the Pension Fund Administrators and Custodians. Sections 3.8 and 4.14 of the transitional guidelines among others, stress the importance of the regulatory functions of the Commission.

If the institutional framework is responsive, another strength of the scheme is its comparative inclusive coverage. Section 3.1 of the guidelines covers all employees in the public service of the Federation, FCT and private sector that have five or more employees.

There is also Strength in the exceptions granted all categories of officers mentioned in Section 291 of the 1999 Constitution as well as the existing pensioners.

Sections 2.19, 2.20, 2.21, 2.22 and 2.23 dealing with NSITF have significantly addressed some of the concerns of NSITF's contributors prior to the new Act.

Sections 3.1, 3.2, 3.3 and 3.4 also partially addressed the plights of employees under the unfunded public sector scheme which had long agitated labour.

There is considerable transparency and accountability consciousness/awareness through compulsory retirement saving accounts and separation of pension funds and assets from the funds and assets of the employers. See section 4.14

Section 4.10 strives to protect the existing gains of the employees where the existing contributions of employers are more than minimum rates as prescribed by the Act.

Sections 1.6 and 1.7 of the Act represent the qualitative strengths of the transitional guidelines in the sense that the guidelines are not presumed closed but open to review while other stakeholders are encouraged to 'exercise their own skill and care in relation to any material contained therein.! This is a good departure from the unhelpful 'take-them-or-go-to-hell' orientation of most official guidelines.

Weaknesses

The guidelines which claim such global outreach are paradoxically silent on states and local government employees. Federalism is founded on minimum standard for all the constituent parts!

Section 3.5 of the guidelines shows the gap between policy formulation and the institutional framework. Why deductions when Pension Funds Administrators and Pension Fund Custodians are not in place?

The scheme is premised on the misplaced assumptions that all employers are rational and accountable such that they would all maintain 'proper books of accounts and records of contributions'. Workers' experience with NSITF does not confirm such optimism.

The minimum equal contributions for both the employers and workers are inequitable. International best practices demand that employers should necessarily pay more.

Guidelines on the NSITF should have made it mandatory for the Fund to make available statements of accounts for contributors under the old scheme within a time frame.

There is no time limit for the payment of the existing pensioners under the guidelines 5.1 and 5.2.

Workers' representation on the Board of the Pen COM is still token.

Threats

- Delay in the registration of the fund Administrators and fund custodians.
- Absence of data base and absolute reliance on government agencies and departments as well as private sector employers to provide information.
- Lack of defined benefits beyond savings.
- Mass ignorance about the provisions of the Act by employees.
- Non-payment of the liabilities of the existing retirees.
- Weak confidence of private sector operators in the capacity of public sector-driven nation-wide pension scheme.
- The limitations of the financial market.
- Inflation environment that erodes benefits.

Opportunities/ Challenges

- To regain the confidence of employees in general and private sector employees in particular.
- To maximise the strengths and minimise (and possibly eliminate!) the identified weaknesses.
- Mass enlightenment of employees about the problems and prospects of the Act and the transitional guidelines.
- Learn from the positive as well as the negative experience of the existing pension schemes.
- Subject the guidelines to continuous reviews until the concerns of all stakeholders are completely addressed.

Conclusion

Labour's view is that the Pen Com as well as other stakeholders must deepen the strengths of the scheme and minimise its weaknesses as identified above. The listed threats should be eliminated while the opportunities and the challenges task the creativity of stakeholders to improve on the scheme and make it sustainable.

The End of Work (II)*

'Job, jobs and jobs are the dividing line in many families between a decent life and a wretched existence' – Nelson MANDELA (1979)

We can as well say farewell to work altogether judging by the resolve of Federal government to soon commence mass retrenchment. Never before have public jobs come under sustained intellectual and doctrinaire assault since Mrs. (Dr.) Ngozi Okonjo-Iweala became the Finance Minister. You wonder what the hell a Finance Ministry and a Finance Minister with World Bank's antecedent (not ILO's antecedent) got to do with job losses or job creation. But that precisely is the problem. It is now part of the fad for the obviously fashionable Dr. Ngozi to convince those that care that as much as 80 per cent of public revenue is unduly spent on civil servants who paradoxically are only one per cent of the population. According to her, the current practice is bad and unsustainable economics. Capital project suffers while civil service is bloated. The sizeable Minister (who certainly should know the burden and joy of size) has repeatedly called for downsizing, sorry, right sizing but 'sizing' of public service nonetheless.

A visit to the federal secretariat on a 'working day' will convince any observer that Minister Ngozi's concern about civil service's idle capacity is far from being misplaced. In fact the current official concern comes rather late than never. A typical secretariat (and Federal Secretariat in particular) passes for an Oshodi market where people in their multitude (and certainly without pretence to some

---

* *Daily Trust*, Monday 22nd December, 2003 pg. 6

orderliness) are buying and selling rather than working and pushing papers and files for common good as envisioned by Marx Weber, the father of modern functioning bureaucracy. We must therefore credit Dr. Ngozi for the common sense. It cannot be and should not in any way be business as usual with respect to public sector employment. The only problem is that we deserve more than common sense from the Honourable Minister. What is needed is real sense about good governance and public sector service delivery. The Minister may be right in balancing budget; through 'right' sizing and retrenchment if idle civil servants but has she balanced the objective of good governance about service delivery by willing hard working civil servants? The issue is that what we actually need is real developmental sense and not just common sense about ration of revenue to number of employed. The promise of NEEDS, of which the respected Minister is the chief driver, is growth and development. With promised growth of 5 to 6 per cent in the next 10 years, Nigeria needs more hands in both public and private sectors of the economy. If we must eradicate illiteracy, halt the scourge of AIDS, build more roads, generate more energy, build more houses to shelter millions of the homeless, then we need more hands to employ to the existing capacity *not* to retrench the existing ones. Thus the real developmental thinking being asked for from our government should be the one that sets to address our potential need rather than the existing common sense that sets to manage our existing current untenable limitation. Yes it is bad enough that we currently have ten drivers to two cars. Current reality underscores wastage and under-capacity utilization. Thus the Minister might be tempted to retrench eight of these drivers to balance the books. But it is lazy and least resistance official economics that sets to balance the books at the expense of balancing objectives of development. Don't we need more drivers even if we currently lack vehicles to engage existing ones, monetization or not? Is the challenge not in getting more vehicles rather than throwing the existing 'excess' drivers out of work? Economics and indeed politics (read: good governance) in a developing economy as ours are about the art of possibilities not art of managing the existing limitation. A population of 130 million people cannot and should not complain that less than a million civil servants are too many, too bloated. On the contrary we need more hands to do urgent jobs. This however does not mean that we cannot frown and even frontally combat the existing inefficiency and gross idle capacity and sheer corruption as expressed in the notorious practice of ghost workforce. We must sack the idle, retrain the re-trainable, re-deploy and relocate workers to where they will add value but let nobody criminalize the public service as if we don't need the service. The chuck of the so-called 80 per cent of resources that goes to the public sector, we all know, does go to the top few public servants that include ministers and the permanent secretaries and NOT the drivers and their likes as such. Even the celebrated corruption of the service is more top-heavy. Thus while we may frown at excess idle drivers, let's not play the legendary ostrich and pretend that we don't need two ministers in any ministry and no less in Ministry of Finance either. By all means let's also do up sizing and not just downsizing, left sizing not just right sizing.

As we are set on the current job cleansing, please let's remember the above Madiba's observation that life is miserable without work. A father or mother sacked means children withdrawn from schools; it means family collapse and starvation. Job-loss is worse than widowhood in the sense that sympathy is not automatic for the former. May the realization of the dire effects of mass sack temper the current lazy official least resistance in governance through proposed mass retrenchment.

Human (Re)Capitalisation[*]

Human capital, though long factored into development discourse attracts less domestic policy attention compared to other factors, such as money capital or land (Abuja plan). CBN, true to its promise, by the weekend released comprehensive, (albeit controversial) guidelines and incentives on consolidation in the banking industry. This is barely a month, CBN governor; Charles Soludo served notice of banking reforms. The speed, the passion and the intensity of banking reform once again underscores the priority of money capital in official policy formulation, which is not bad, if same position is applicable in other areas begging for attention.

The point however, cannot be overemphasised that what is good for the banks (money capital) is also good for human capital. "People are the real wealth of nations" aptly observed 2004 UNDP Human Development Report. Refreshingly too, National Economic Empowerment and Development Strategy (NEEDS) and its state versions, SEEDS are loud in their commitment to the PEOPLE (human capital). United Nations Millennium Development Goals (MDGs) to which Nigeria is also a signatory among 189 countries are profoundly about human capital with clear-cut agenda to eradicate poverty, promote human dignity and global peace.

Notwithstanding the above, policy rhetorics about the importance of human capital fly in the face of increasing human capital degradation in Nigeria. By all means, the misery index of the banks namely; asset-liability mismatch, capital inadequacy, weak internal controls, fraud and poor management, call for urgent actions such as re-capitalisation. But the human capital indexes are no less

---

[*] *Daily Trust* Monday 9th August, 2004

miserable. According to UNDP 2004 Development, Nigeria is among the poorest of the poor in Human Development Index (HDI). A country which once proudly ranked high in per-capital income, literacy and life expectancy in the 1970s and 1980s, is today at the lowest level not thanks to "unprecedented reversals" of the 1990s. It is a sad commentary that Nigeria ranks 151, only rivalled by Sierra Leone, Mauritania and Haiti in low human development with life expectancy at 51 years, compared to Algeria 69 years. Nigeria with per capital of 860 dollars compared to South Africa's 10,070. As we are envious of South Africa's "mega-banks", let's remember the country's mega per-capital income, "mega adult literacy rate of 86% compared to Nigeria's 66.8%. Put in another way, given the direct relationship between human development indexes (as it were) and growth, it's time we accorded human capital formation the same priority as money capital. The experience of CBN so far with banks' consolidation shows that if there is the will, there must be the way out.

First, human capital is too important to be left to our doctrinaire unhelpful market forces. We need an emergency, through affirmative state interventionist policy actions to urgently combat poverty, put an end to illiteracy and ignorance (the recent worst manifestation being Okija notorious murderous shrines) and reverse the current human destitution.

Secondly, there must be time frame to eradicate poverty just as there is time frame for "mergers" and "acquisition" of banks. The bane of poverty discourse is that it is seemingly endless. "Poverty alleviation" entered our lexicon in late 80s, when the human casualties of IMF/World Bank's favoured SAP are too many and too grim to be ignored. Remember SAP 'riots'. Two decades after, countries like Cuba and Chile (a country with scores of SAP riots too) have eradicated absolute poverty. We have however shamelessly turned poverty reduction into an endless process under the notorious Poverty Redirection Process (PRPS). Let's see human recapitalization plan NOT gory picture of human cannibalization as Okija's. Poverty reduction must be time-bound just like there is time limit for bank reform.

Thirdly, to enhance human re-capitalisation, we must think beyond the existing poverty paradigm. We remain poor, because we think poor even as we act rich (sorry, big brotherly). It's time to generate wealth through human capital application of industrial productivity and motivation. Bank of Industry (BOI) must do for industries what CBN is doing for the banks. BOI must come out with revival plan to bail out hundreds of distressed industries, so that the existing huge idle human capital in forms of unemployment and underemployment can be put into active use.

Lastly, there is an urgent need for all inclusive compassion. Same kind of compassion extended to bank staff expected to lose out in wake of bank reform must be extended to thousands of workers already threatened with sack in the public sector. Real compassion must even start with job-losses prevention and not sack through redeployment, retraining and even amnesty for previous past records. Social safety net should be all-inclusive. Refreshing that CBN promises to work with Bankers' Committee to "assist staff that will be disengaged to access SMIEIS fund to set up their own SMES and consequently create "jobs and wealth". What similar plan does Finance Minister, Okonjo Iweala have for working with workers unions in the public sector who are being threatened with job-losses on account of reform? What is good for the banks must necessarily not be bad for other sectors of the economy.

Pope John Paul II, Labour Dimension[*]

What did the late Chief Rotimi Williams share in common with the late Pope John Paul II? Yours sincerely was tidying up his dedication notes on the late legal icon when the death of the Pope was announced. Every discernable observer agrees that longevity and hard work were the trademarks of the duo and other few living legends like Nelson Mandela and Fidel Castro who in their eighties are enthusiastically putting in efforts for humanity. Comparing anybody with saintly Pope definitely makes imagination run riot. But that was precisely what the late Pope's deeds and words conveyed; tasks our imagination to do away with the unthinking mindset of disconnect between the spirituality and practical deeds.

No Pope in recent times had given Christianity practical expressions than Pope John Paul II. He was in the Mosque and Synagogue without ranking them less in significance to the Church. Did this singular gesture make any difference to our 'Christian' and 'Islamic' warlords erecting Berlin Walls between indivisible faiths? The Pope stoutly condemned the war in Iraq no less than he condemned terror as means of politics. Joseph Stalin during the Second World War reportedly asked how many troops the then Pope had. Watching millions that mourned Paul II, there can be little doubt that moral power is far more potent than the bombs.

We saw nothing, learnt nothing from Pope's legendary life if the singular lesson in fusion of religious labels and religious deeds escapes our imagination. After Nelson Mandela's, who else does his life and words make such impact on humanity like the late Pope? Whose funeral would command such cross-cutting potpourri that

---

[*] *Daily Trust*, Monday 18th April, 2005

included Iran's President Khatami and Israel's Sharon on one hand and Tony Blair and Robert Mugabe on the other hand? Cuba's Fidel Castro who had led hundreds of mass rallies against Uncle Sam's constant aggression reportedly led another mass rally of Cuban faithful praying for the dying Pope. Some incurable unthinking ideologues repeated the same old outworn trite that '...communism collapsed headlong during the pontificate of the Polish Pope'. Judging by the religious practical deeds of the Pope, it is charitable to say he built real classless community of nations (in spite of communists) than to credit him with some ideological triumph. He cultivated commonwealth of global goodwill, which betrays the empty rhetoric of British Commonwealth, the wealth that is getting uncommon every second.

Pope reportedly did his last mass from his sickbed. Pope's devotion to service even at the age of 84 confirms the validity of Yoruba saying; *Ojo iku lojo isinmi* (Only death guarantees eternal rest). Pope added value to the last minute, just as Rotimi Williams did. Today, employers hire and fire at will under the notorious flexi-work policy. The only thing constant is insecurity of work. Is there any lesson for governments and employers alike from Papal example of security of tenure? Over the years, we had criminalized long service through arbitrary service purges (so called reforms), through downsizing and silly peg on years of active service (35 years of service or 50 years of age). The unhelpful policy that sees labour as a cost item in the market place which must be cut at all costs had led to early mass retirement, mass retrenchment, loss of value addition and experience to the detriment of the nation's human resources development. In the absence of social security and pension schemes we have witnessed pauperization of retirees such that, the army of unpaid pensioners constitutes the poorest of the new poor.

Don't get me wrong. No employer should keep a worker a day longer who is incapable of adding value whether young or old. Conversely no worker should stay an extra day on job if she or he realises that work is less useful both in terms of earnings and productivity. However a doctrinaire cost-saving strategy that criminalises labour on account of reducing cost as favoured by IMF and World Bank (whose staffs paradoxically are assured of secured mouth watering tenure) is as ungodly as it is inconsistent with Pope's lesson in longevity. It is sheer market farce to celebrate or throw away labour force as a policy.

President Obasanjo's anti-corruption crusade is unsustainable unless mass employment is combined with job retention and job longevity/security is matched with social\security and sustainable pension scheme. The fear of job-losses and destitution after work is the beginning of graft/corruption consciousness.

Abundance of wisdom however lies more in Pope Paul II's quotable quotes which must task the conscience of the politicians and international mangers of labour. We cannot mouth respect for the Pope and disrespect his words and deeds. An advocate of decent work long before ILO's advocacy, Pope tasked us to 'Ask not whether a man is useful in his work but whether the work is useful to him'. He described trade unions 'a mouthpiece for the struggle for social justice'. How many mourners share this Papal perspective? Here in Nigeria on the eve of Pope's burial President Obasanjo signed the labour bill to law. That Act is worse in provisions and penalties than colonial Trade Union Ordinance of 1930s. It does not see unions as mouthpiece for the struggle for social justice as Papacy favoured, but agent of destabilization that must be tamed through draconian clauses. Strikes in health, banking and air transport sectors among others are prohibited with jail sentences for a breach. The labour Act is a reminiscent of restrictive decree in communist Poland which Lech Walesa's Solidarity independent and free trade union resisted with the support of the late Pope.

Pope John Paul II once questioned the validity of economic orthodoxy that elevates economic fundamentals (external reserves, GDP, inflation rates, etc.) above human welfare. According to him 'A just wage for the worker is the ultimate test of whether any economic system is performing justly'.

Rethinking Labour - I[*]

May Day is over but the spectre of labour hunts nonetheless. The bane of labour discourse is that we often labour to discuss labour in some narrow 'labour terms'. Labour is 'analysed' almost in relations to strikes, wage increase, resistance against obnoxious government policies. Labour hits the headlines with every work-stoppage such that few remember that in the absence of a provider state (power failure, water shortages, etc.) only labour keeps the country moving. Some unionists have not transcended this narrow-definition of labour's purpose either. The recent strike (or was it a blackmail?) by petroleum tankers' drivers underscores how negative application of strike weapon begets negativity in labour discourse and labour's perception.

Government that should know better and fashion out broader labour policy is also hooked on this parochialism, as it were. Labour has been frozen to some troublesomeness; all needed to be done is to curtain it. The discredited colonialist thesis of 'lazy' African worker has been reinvented under an IMF neo-liberal dogma to justify downsizing of mass of civil servants even when there is official recognition that the private sector labour absorption is constrained if not foreclosed. The results; mass unemployment and value-subtraction at a time when there is much work to be done and the nation is begging for growth and development. In the absence of social security, the attendant poverty takes us far away from the Millennium Development Goals (MDGs). NEEDS promises 7million new jobs but we are counting loses of the existing few thousands jobs than we are talking of jobs' retention and job

* *Daily Trust*, Monday 2nd May, 2005

creation. Wastage of its oil revenue totalling billions of dollars has captured imagination worldwide. But no nation has encouraged the wastage of human asset like Nigeria through scourge war policy of zero-motivation, low return on efforts and disenabling environment for productivity. The British High Commissioner was charitable to describe the country as a huge 'visa industry'. Stripped of its diplomatic sugar coating, I guess he meant Nigeria is the only country that encourages Trans-Atlantic labour trade centuries after slavery was abolished. Results of both slavery and 'visa industry' are the same; brain drain. We discussed resource control only in relations to non-renewable resources like crude oil, solid minerals when enlightened peoples of the world know that the major resource is human resource.

The latest fall-out of the labour curtailment policy is the new labour Act that sets to among others decentralize trade union centres (read: NLC), prohibits strikes in health and education sectors. Governments at all level, employers and workers are encouraged to critically rethink the role of labour and trade unions in national development.

The motto of NLC reads: Labour Creates Wealth. This means trade unions are conscious of their responsibility beyond the trouble –making function attributed to them. Every employer or investor knows that of all the factors of production human resource is the most important. Indeed the key to the success stories of countries like China, Japan, Malaysia and India is the creative manner labour has been motivated and mobilized for unprecedented growth and development. These countries lack non-renewable resources like crude oil but are nonetheless abundantly blessed with human resources in quantity and quality as in China. Successive Nigerian governments have been unable to appreciate the role of labour as a source of wealth that needs to be cultivated for development through a defined structure of incentives, training and retraining, involvement in decision making processes and organizational building. Economic recovery will elude Nigeria until it stops treating labour at arms length.

British colonial authority appreciated the centrality of labour in development. The first ministry it created was Department of Labour in 1914. That singular Ministry played a critical role in mobilising the 'natives' for colonial development that included the building of railway lines. Today Ministry of Finance has assumed inexplicable ascendancy as we have almost reduced development to budgeting (or is it budget cut?) 'cost-saving' measures (right-sizing) and book keeping at the expense of broader objective of development, which is wealth generation and peoples' welfare. By the way, when last did you hear about National Man--power Board? So much for human resource planning and development in the age of Procurement and Due process.

President Woodrow Wilson of United States (1913) said 'the great struggling unknown masses of the men who are at the base of everything are the dynamic force that is lifting the levels of society. A nation is as great, and only as great, as her rank and file'. In a similar vein, Vice- President Walter Fredrick Mondale under Carter Administration (1977-1981) remarked that 'we have the most wealth of any nation because our workers have the skill to create it. We have the best products because they know how to make them. We have the most democratic system because of the values our trade unions have to sustain it'. Whence the quotable quotes of our leaders underscoring the significance of workers in nation's development?

The new Labour Act is informed by the same unhelpful labour curtailment strategy that has de-motivated and divided labour and invariably undermined growth and development of the country. Coming from Mr. President who had seen the futility of balkanized labour and its adverse impact for development prior to 1978 once again shows our capacity for one-step forward, many steps backward. All in a lifetime. Mr. President has just returned from his historic long, long Asian tours. How many trade union centres does China have? How many does Vietnam have? Chinese authorities know that you cannot easily mobilise atomised trade unions for development, which explains the existence of monopoly union centre in China. Assuming we attribute one labour centre to communist system of China, what do we say of the capitalist Western countries that long knew that decentralization was unhelpful to development?

Governments in USA and Britain know that labour is a critical market actor that is better managed through a monopoly centres just as businesses or capital. In USA there is only one labour centre, AFL-CIO while in Britain, TUC. The EU is forging common market as much as it is encouraging one indivisible pan-European labour centre. Worldwide, labour is cultivated by enlightened governments as partner in development.

The role of one indivisible labour force even assumes special importance. In a country in which ethnicity and religious jingoism had taken a centre stage, to further balkanize labour, the remaining pillar of unity is to make mockery of the daily rooftop sermon that the unity of Nigeria is not negotiable. You already bargain the unity of the country when you officially facilitate atomisation of an institution of labour market like a pan-Nigerian labour organization.

Pension: beyond verifications*

The bane of pension administration in the past had been poor record keeping. It was therefore refreshing that National Pension Commission (PENCOM) devoted the significant part of the month of April to verify claimant- pensioners as part of the process of clearing the backlog of arrears owned the country's senior workers. Better late than never. The principle of verifications cannot be disputed even if the details of the process are as controversial as the pension crisis itself. The real pensioners are the first causalities when records are grossly distorted and patently inadequate. In fact "ghost" claimants cornered what is meant for the legitimate pensioners, no thanks to untidy records. The strength of the recent exercise lies in insistence for once on basic bio-matrix which included fingerprints, passports and scanning of original letters of employment, promotion and retirements among others. With 111 designated centres nation-wide and over 300 computers, the verification exercise had a global outreach. Given the fact that pensioners' verification is not part of its original core mandate, PENCOM's application of new best practices to pension administration, with respect to documentation and transparency must necessarily add value to the naughty process of resolution of pension crisis in the country. The recent exercise also put to test the capacity of public agencies to collaborate. The pitfall of pension administration in the past has been uncoordinated and disjointed activities of varying agencies expected to work in unison. The verification exercise remarkably brought together the Federal and state pension boards as well as pension departments of military, police in collaborative pension work. The hope is that if the relevant

---

* *Daily Trust*, 8th May 2006

pension agencies work together, pensioners would not be denied their legitimate earnings individually. In the past precisely because the pension administrators operated separately, pensioners were unfairly cheated separately. Better still, all relevant pension agencies working together are better than an agency suffocating under the weight of a clear cut collective burden which public pension administration has inadvertently turned into. The verification exercise is therefore a test case of service delivery by public agencies.

Another significant feature of the verification exercise is the practical application of public-private sector partnership. The involvement of banks to pay the certified pensioners is a radical departure from the old method of public pay masters characterized by sundry malpractices.

Paradoxically the strength of the verification exercise also brought to the fore its weaknesses. For one, collaborative work makes sense if every agency adds value in the true sense of the word. The truth is that records of the past by previous federal and state agencies though completely not useless hardly help matters. In any case, if all were in order verification exercise was hardly necessary in the first place. Also there was a seeming underestimation of the crisis of confidence engendered by the past pension mal- administration. Thus while PENCOM put in place some logistics for the pensioners it was debatable if it was enough to assuage the sheer understandable desperation of the depressed pensioners. Even far more important is the seemingly slow service delivery by the accredited banks saddled with the responsibility to pay the pensioners. Thus after many pensioners were duly verified the promised cheques did not come or reportedly came pretty late.

The challenge for PENCOM and other relevant agencies is to quickly eliminate the threat to the quick resolution of the pension crisis characterized by arrears of pensioners' claims. The verification exercise should never be treated again as a uniform event that must be done with at a given time at all places. It must be treated as a process with graduated schedules such that there is a gradual improvement on each exercise at different places. Private sector involvement in pension management is meaningless unless it improves on where public sector management fails. Therefore PENCOM should only select private sector operators that are conscious of their corporate and social responsibility. Beyond verification, the real challenge is to truly put behind us the crisis of pensioners' compensation and this is not possible until we put in place a sustainable process and very urgently too until we clear the outstanding arrears of genuine and verified claimants. With the best of arrangement, it must be clear that the amount made available to PENCOM can only pay for one month out of average arrears six months. Thus with the best of arrangement, PENCOM and all other relevant pension agencies are only managing poverty with all its attendant crisis of expectations. In the agencies deserve our sympathy and understanding than condemnation. This is why the call by NLC on May Day that Mr President sets aside 1 billion dollars from the external reserves to clear the pensions' arrears is worthy thought for food. And think about it; if Nigeria can issue a cheque to pay few creditors in Paris club a whopping sum of $12 billion, a miserable percentage of that sum to pay those who labour for the country can certainly not be too much. If there is the will there will always be some ways anyway!

May Day and 2007 Polls[*]

We are living in an interesting time of political transition with all its controversies and challenges. This year's May Day understandably assumed a special importance. Taking place against the background of a democratic transition, the critical question is; of what relevance is labour to Nigeria's 2007 transition process? Globally the debate had long shifted from the unhelpful and uncritical question as to whether labour had a role to play in a political process or not to a more useful perspective on what and how labour could participate in political process. So much for the deceit of the money bags and their agents who on the one hand are openly and unapologetically deeply involved in politics but on the other hand discourage labour from participating beyond being called upon dust their voters' card for new set of corrupt exploiters every four years. With all their limitations, trade unions, more than any organization and business concerns are formidable democratic organizations that have a lot to offer in a democratic dispensation. An American frontline unionist, Lane Kirkland, long observed that "Unions can no more live without democracy than a fish without water." Bjorn Beckman is one Swedish political economist that has done extensive original works on trade union performance in Nigeria. According to him, 'expressing dissent, organising alternative opinions, challenging those in power, and contesting for office are all central features of a democratic process'. His conclusion is that Nigerian trade unions in Nigeria have passed democratic test which is a loud lesson for the larger society. In a country in which parties and party formations

---

[*] The Daily Trust, 7th May 2007

were once long prohibited by the military, only unions were true vehicles for democratic expression at work places and larger society. Unions held periodic elections, removed elected leaders and routinely re-elected new ones at a time it was clearly unpopular to do so. Democracy seems fashionable today, but democracy has been the bedrock of functional trade union movement in the country.

As recent as February this year, NLC organised its 9th Delegates' Conference, just as it organized 8th Delegates' confab in 2003 and 7th conference in 1999. Nigeria marches on the road to the 4th Republic 42 years after Independence. But NLC has inaugurated 9 elected executive leaderships in the past 30 years of its formation (using the restructuring of 1978 as a bench-mark!). The celebrated "civilian" to "civilian" transition hitherto a jinx for larger Nigeria had been a passing fad for trade union movement.

The recently concluded conference of NLC was adjudged by local and international observers that included Council of South African Trade Unions (COSATU), Organization of African Trade Union Unity, OATUU, International Trade Union Congress (ITUC), Canadian Labour Congress (CLC), and International Labour Organization (ILO) among numerous others. Democratic best practice that took place at NLC national level was replicated at the states levels. Remarkable was that the defeated challengers in labour elections accepted the outcome of the contest. Election was not perceived as "a do or die" affairs. Losers congratulated winners. Similarly in the true spirit of union solidarity, the winners extended hands of cooperation and solidarity to the losers. No ballot-snatching, late arrivals of materials and plain outright inventions of election results as we witnessed in the past three weeks of elections conducted by INEC. Labour has further advanced the cause of democracy, through active engagement of politicians to refocus them from mutually destructive preoccupation of politics of persons to mutually rewarding issue-centred politics. Labour has also long appreciated that politics is too important to be left for the politicians alone. As part of the age long desire of labour to be politically relevant, NLC together with progressive forces formed and registered Party for Social Democracy (PSD). The party later changed to Labour Party (LP). LP, is one fastest growing party in the country. It made significant impact in a number of states, the notable being Edo, Ondo, Lagos and Oyo states. With remarkable number of elected MPs in the states, LP has quantitatively enriched the political space.

All the above rich democratic heritage and best practices position labour to be able to critically assess the recently held elections in the country. Nobody, Labour inclusive contemplated the wholesome electoral malfeasance of the recent times. INEC's performance does not in any way represent national historic best democratic practices. The defence of Professor Maurice Iwu with his generous self pass mark was purely academic and self-serving. For a nation that started with robust democracy at Independence, with rich history in elections, the most celebrated being June 12 1993 election, 2007 election could be better conducted given the unprecedented mass enthusiasm. Observers, who routinely hail elections of mass organizations such as NLC elections in February, have been made to uncharitably talk down on Nigeria because of INEC's despicable performance.

What then should be done after flawed elections, the fall-out of which still hunts the nation like a spectre? If there was no May-Day, the main opposition party leaders could have invented one. They fixed their protest for May-Day. Many labour watchers thought opposition was rather opportunistic in their choice of protest date. This might not be surprising given that opportunism is a variant of politics in this part of the world. The seemingly cold response the protesting politicians got however says something about the mass perception of the democratic credentials of the opposition. Labour deployed the flawed process of the recent weeks but was not excited either by the new opposition "democrats" who for once suddenly discovered the importance of May-Day, as a protest day just because they have been declared elections losers. Many recalled that Proverbial water has passed under the bridge since Vice President Atiku once declared labour a "threat" to democracy because labour dared to patriotically protest the obnoxious petroleum price increases policy of Obasanjo administration of which he was a notable partner.

It's time for a completely paradigm shift with respect to the notion of power retention and power application by politicians.

President Olusegun Obasanjo spent the last eight years in exercising power as a do or die affair mainly in favour of the rich, the strong and even the wicked as in Ibadan. Regrettably many other political actors followed uncritically including notable opposition leaders who have miserably lost out in the ruthless race of the might is right. To be humble and honest in office-seeking and office retention and extend solidarity and support to others including opponents had been sadly seen as a weakness rather than strength. In the process, we have witnessed conquest in place of genuine democratic contest. The on-going shameless impeachment process against Deputy Governor Femi Pedro by Governor Bola Tinubu is the Lagos worse version of discredited do or die politics in which might is ever right. The political class must cultivate a new notion of power for the service of the majority and minority alike. Paradoxically it is the President-elect, Umar Yar'Adua that has so far challenged the polity with alternative political body and mouth languages that approximate this desired paradigm shift. While Maurice Iwu talked as an arrogant triumphant winner in elections he was supposed to be an umpire, the President-elect heals the wounds of the nation by envisaging electoral reform. Asked by BBC about his attitude to INEC declaration as a winner of a controversial election, Yar'Adua denied excitement citing with humility the challenges of energy crisis, educational and health decay ahead. His May-Day's hands of friendship to the oppressed and the poor that labour represents could serve as a great motivation for labour in the great task for economic recovery. Yours comradely is yet to read opposition May-Day solidarity message even as they chose May Day for protest. Trevor Clark entitled his great volume on Late Alhaji Sir Tafawa Balewa, *A Right Honourable Gentleman*. That was the age in which to be gentle, extend courtesies, be humble while remaining principled and discipline was a virtue. What do our present-day politicians want to be remembered for?

Strike as an Acid Test[*]

'Who struggles can fail. Who doesn't struggle has already failed!'
- Berrolt Brecht (1809-1956) German poet.

My dear brother, Monsieur Olusegun Adeniyi, Special Adviser to President Yar'Adua on Communication has brought some colour to Uphill (read: Aso Rock) communication mill. In recent past, special assistants (SAs) on President's Media affairs had cultivated the notorious image of glorified messengers completely detached from the top-down messages they paradoxically strived hard to ram down on the populace. Many SAs delivered disinterestedly. Certainly not few SAs in a non-creative manner almost by rout delivered apparently the same way the messages were dictated to them. It is a refreshing departure from the recent I-Am-Directed unthinking rule to read Adeniyi's official reflection on the just suspended three-day national Strike. Precisely because yours sincerely was involved, I bear witness to say it takes some capacity, independence and conviction for Olusegun to develop notes in the heat of a national strike with a view of conveying the official perspective on the strike as published in most yesterday's Sunday papers. I dare bet that like other SAs Adeniyi was certainly directed. However his efforts at delivery and the Value Added Tasks, VAT (more than 10percent indeed!) in his documentations, analysis and value judgment convey some deep interestedness and ownership of official government approach to the strike. As remarkable as Adeniyi's account is, it however regrettably reflects government views and government views alone. Making a

---

* *The Daily Trust*, 25th June 2007

83

good official case can however only be meaningful and credible if the other unofficial concerns which in the in the first instance trigger the crisis are factored into analysis. Naughty issue like a national strike tasks official capacity for holistic analysis that can and should inform policies.

The truth of the matter is that the recently suspended strike was an acid test for the nation. It is a good commentary that all the stakeholders, in particular labour and government, did not conclusively proved this singular dangerous test as so designed by the outgoing administration. For the first time the nation was faced with the naughty challenge of coping with the policy landmines planted by an outgoing administration. The twin policies of increase in the prices of petroleum products and Value Added Taxes (VAT) at the tail end of Obasanjo administration were policy provocations that could only lead to anything but peace as we just witnessed. Adeniyi was hard put to convince anybody that Obasanjo administration did its successor a favour by taking the "flak for the unpopular but necessary decision" via fuel price and VAT hike. With three day- national strikes, millions of human hour loss and billions of naira loss due to lack of production, it is an open knowledge that Obasanjo government truly punished Nigerians, even after leaving the office. One does not need a conspiracy theory either to accept that the outgoing government acted as agent provocateur by handing over policies that provoked strikes and protests. Conversely it is to the eternal credit of Nigerians including Yar'Adua government that the resolution of the crisis was not done in favour of the preference of the departed Obasanjo regime but in line with the possible wishes and preferences of Nigerians. Far from the ideal of preferred policy reversal, the agreement between labour and government was still nonetheless a win-win one. The agreement confirms the poetic insight of Brecht that there is wisdom in resistance against obnoxious policies past or present. Those who struggle can fail but those who rationalise and are complacent to dare resistance had only accepted failure. Both labour and the new government of Yar'Adua in recent days struggled against inherited burden with a successful win-win and not failed outcome. The Nigeria Labour Congress (NLC) under its new President, Comrade Abdulwaheed Omar together with TUC commendably kept faith with inherited culture of resistance under Adams Oshiomhole. Indeed NLC and TUC delivered unprecedented deal that included zero increases on VAT, diesel and kerosene and significantly too implementation of approved 15 per cent wage increase with effective implementation from January. In the same breadth it is important to commend Yar'Adua government for daring to struggle in the face of labour's resistance against policies that were done by its predecessor with utter disregard for due process and public welfare. Segun Adeniyi accepts as much that VAT 100 per cent hike was an abuse of budgetary process and the arbitrary postponement of wage increase payment further confirms the impunity of the old regime. If there had not been resistance of the last few days the benefit of discovery of untidy process could have been denied the nation.

The events of last week show that Nigeria has the chance of returning to civility. The self righteous posturing of the past with utter disregard for process should give way to correct policy formulation process that calls for mass consultation. Regardless of the strike which was clearly avoidable, recent events show that meaningful contestation and cooperation between the government and the governed is the key to good governance.

Reinventing Decent Mass Employment[*]

"A lot of fellows nowadays have a B.A., M.D., or Ph.D. unfortunately, they don't have a J.O.B" - *Antonio Dominio, Singer and song writer*

Michael Imoudu National Institute for Labour Studies (MINILS), Ilorin under its dynamic Director/Chief Executive, John Olarewaju kept faith with its annual Labour-Summit programme last week. The 4th edition of the Labour Summit held at the newly commissioned MINILS' Resource Centre on the 6th of December Thursday at Ilorin. The summit with the timely theme: Furthering National Development Through Decent Work Strategies rightly put employment issues back to national and international discourse. Decent Work concept accepts special importance for Nigeria at this critical period of its development. It assumes promotion of freely chosen productive employment. The assumption that informs this is that promoting employment opportunities for a country is fundamental to decent work. Decent Work Agenda (DWA) insists that we must place employment at the heart of economic and social policies and development. In fact full employment should be the means and the end of growth and development of a country. There is official lip service to employment generation but the reality is that Nigeria is among the few countries that International Labour Organization (ILO) has singled out as countries that have recorded jobless growth. In the past eight years Nigeria talks of average growth rate of 6-7%. However, this growth rate goes side by side with massive unemployment rate which is as high as 35%. In fact

---

[*] *The Daily Trust,* 10th December 2007

86

with mass unemployment the concept of Decent Work sounds unavoidable luxury. The assumption of DWA is that there are already jobs; all we need is to make the jobs decent through adequate compensation and genuine social security. But you cannot talk of decency of jobs where there are no jobs. DWA is both about quantity and quality of jobs but the reality is that in Nigeria the quantity is not even there and talking about quality jobs sounds Greek not Nigerian.

Recently the Federal Ministry of Labour came out with a report on Repositioning the Federal Ministry of Labour for Vision 2020. The report is very graphic about state of unemployment. Witness this: "While mass unemployment, especially among school leavers and graduates of tertiary institutions, presents a crisis, lack of material support and even skills underline the dearth of empowerment among certain segments of the society. The vulnerable segment of the Nigeria society, comprising youths, women and the disabled, do not only lack jobs, they equally do not have the capacity to contribute to society at large."

The point cannot be overstated that the singular factor in the current spread of poverty is idle capacity, mass unemployment and gross underemployment of mass number of people willing to work but could simply not get jobs. Conversely the only way to halt the exiting race to the bottom by a multitude that live bellow a dollar per day is to provide jobs, jobs and jobs for the critical mass.

Against the background of officially acknowledged mass unemployment due to retrenchment and serial closures of labour intensive industries like textile industry for instance the expectation is that the inaugural budget of President Musa Yar'Adua will frontally address the issue of employment generation. Alas as yours sincerely has pointed out this budget is *employment shy* with without necessarily admitting as much. 2008 Budget operates within the same unhelpful paradigm of oil and gas revenue sharing, which paradoxically has been the bane of Nigeria's economy. A budget that operates within the context of the 7-point agenda that favours Wealth generation among others, what happens to industrial capacity utilization and clear-cut job creation targets? There is certainly no framework to

87

hold this budget accountable about how it would revive the fast collapsing real sector when it does not set boosted capacity utilization as a target. Sadly the debate at the national assembly over the budget so far has not shown that this country appreciates the gravity of the current mass unemployment and mass idle capacity in the face of pressing needs of 140 million people. Due to the government policies of privatisation, commercialisation, restructuring, rightsizing, factory closures and severances, hundreds of thousands of direct jobs have been as well as millions of indirect jobs. In place we now have various forms of indecent unsustainable jobs that include *okada* riding, and street vendors. Due to the government policies of privatisation, commercialisation, restructuring, rightsizing, factory closures and severances, hundreds of thousands of direct jobs have been and millions of indirect jobs. Who will reinvent these jobs?

The concept of decent work also underscores fundamental rights at work, the notable ones sanctioned by ILO Conventions No. 87 and 98 that guarantee workers' right to freely organize and engage in collective bargaining. Other fundamental rights are freedom from discrimination, from forced or child labour. Significantly decent work holds that there must be adequate returns on efforts i.e. that there must be adequate incomes from work with income floor like minimum wage as well as social floor like security of social protection. Today, contrary to the principle of decent work, labour is still being treated like a commodity to be bought and dispensed with. Even at that: as a commodity, Nigeria's labour is the most lowly prized compared to other factors of production like capital. Capital market is more attractive because of higher rate of return therein compared to labour market which is miserably depressed.

In spite of the effort of trade unions to improve on the wages of workers through collective bargaining, we are still far from the ideal of living wage. In fact there is the new working poor whose salaries and wages can hardly take them to work not to talk of taking them home. All the issues inherent in decent work agenda point to the character and the nature of Nigeria's development agenda. It's time we interrogated the vision that rightly wants to make Nigeria one of the leading 20 economies by 2020. What makes an economy "big"? The issue is not the bigness of the economy whether now or at some later dates in 2020. The critical success factor is the nature and character of the economy. Is it a job-led economy or job-less economy? Is the economy sustainable, productive and industrial built on value-adding manufacturing activities and mass employment as it is in India and China or extractive, import-consuming, smuggling driven, unemployment driven like Nigeria? Government must critically re-look at the current neo-liberal policies of deregulation and trade liberalization which have led to factory closures and income poverty.

It is the government through macro-economic policies, dealing with interest rate, exchange rate, regulatory framework as well as leadership by examples that give direction for private sector to follow. Private sector may be the engine of growth but it is the government that provides for and oils this engine of growth. We must reaffirm the contribution stable and quality jobs make to a healthy economy and just and equal communities by implementing inclusive strategies for full and productive employment, including for those currently working in the so-called informal economy that need rights and justice to defend their interests. All people have the right to work, to good working conditions and to sufficient income for their basic economic, social and family needs, a right that should be enforced by providing mass and sustainable jobs as well as adequate living wages.

Teachers' Strike and Servant Leadership[*]

Public primary and secondary schools have been shut down for over a week. Critical mass of our pupils and students are out of schools on account of the ongoing avoidable strike. Many of them expected to write their external examinations, namely NECO and WAEC are now roaming the streets.

Teachers have given the notice of their resolve to exercise their legitimate right to picket private schools in furtherance of their demands and in the knowledge that an injury to one (public school) is also an injury to another (private school). If they do, the nation then faces the prospect of nationwide schools shutdown.

The three facets of the education system, namely primary, secondary and tertiary are interrelated. Paralysis of primary and secondary schools means that the polytechnics, universities as well as sundry colleges of education are under threat too. How we resolve the compensation crisis in the primary and secondary schools will determine how we face up to the similar challenges in the tertiary institutions. Already, some polytechnic lecturers are reported to have gone on strike.

Of course, it is an open knowledge that the pay crisis in the university system is far from over. The danger therefore is that once the teachers' strike degenerates, we may be inadvertently deepening the crisis in the entire educational sector. The latent impact of the crisis is even grimmer for the nation. Compared to other countries at similar stage of development and with same resource endowment, such as Malaysia, India, China, Indonesia, Nigeria has poorer educational output and leaning outcomes.

* *Daily Trust* Monday July 7, 2008

Our educational outcomes are dismal. Primary and secondary enrolments are still very low. While Rwanda that is coming out of war of genocide has recorded primary school enrolment as high as 98 per cent, Nigeria's primary school enrolment is still less than 50 per cent. In the North, the figure is even less than the national average.

With respect to secondary school enrolment, the picture is bad. Only 25% of girls and 29% of boys are in secondary schools at ordinary time. As a matter of fact, Nigeria's education sector has taken a leap backward with the re-emergence of new critical mass of illiterates who for whatever reasons are simply out of school.

Without the ongoing strike, therefore, Nigeria was already in near disaster and emergency situation with respect to educational output and quality. The NUT's on-going strike is therefore a welcome reminder and indeed a wake-up call for all stakeholders to address the educational crisis, which one of the manifestations is low pay for teachers.

Despite the seeming disagreement between NUT and the Federal Government on how to resolve the crisis, what is clear is that everybody agrees that teachers deserve better pay. There is also consensus that we cannot drive the educational reform agenda on the back of ill-motivated working teachers. The devil is in the details of how to get the pay of teachers' right and not in the desirability of teachers' demands.

Rather than the Federal Government threatening to deal with the striking teachers if they carry out their legitimate action of picketing private schools, let the Federal Government deploy all its mandate and resources to meet the teachers' demands. The fundamental issue here is improved pay for all teachers in return for urgent mass school enrolment and improved service delivery.

President Umaru Yar'Adua singled out Human Capital Development as one of the 7-point critical development success factors of his administration. The NUT strike and the issues therein complement the president's same desire to fix the education crisis and indeed both the government and NUT must work together to halt educational decline.

It is regrettable that President Yar'Adua who commendably raised the hope of a labour-friendly administration under the banner of servant-leadership is sliding into the unhelpful do-nothing conflicting labour relations of the OBJ regime. President Yar'Adua's government has handled knotty hard issues like fuel pricing with relative maturity, sensitivity and understanding than his predecessor. By keeping with the spirit and content of the agreement with NLC with respect to petroleum pricing, the government has maintained sanity and peace in the petroleum downstream sector.

What is sauce for the petroleum downstream sector is certainly sauce in greater measure for the education sector. President Yar'Adua has commendably increased the budgetary allocation to education even though it was still far from the 26 per cent global average. But it was a bold move in the 2008 budget proposal that monetary votes to education should increase. Happily too, the National Assembly has appropriated enough funds in the present budget to meet the federal component of the teachers' demand.

President Umaru Yar'Adua is therefore urged to offer necessary leadership by directing a circular authorising the payment of teachers on federal payroll. The government has the will and capacity to address the compensation. It is in favour of the teachers in return for it, service delivery and discipline on the part of teachers. President Yar'Adua should do what he has commendably done for the power sector emergency with education sector. He should urgently mobilise the governors by constructively engaging them to guarantee improved pay for teachers.

In addition, the Governors' Forum under the leadership of Governor Bukola Saraki must urgently intervene and return the Federal Government and teachers to the path of dialogue and conflict resolution. We dare not subject the critical issues like education, health, labour pay, etc. The Teachers Salary Structure (TSS) being demanded by the NUT is part of the necessary minimum standard for us to reinvent the education sector.

Happily, many state governors in their own right have improved on teachers' pay in the knowledge that they can only retain good teaching hands with good pay. If we combine the recent scandalous national power meltdown, Niger Delta chaos, industry collapse, and mass unemployment with complete school shutdown, we are inadvertently providing the acid test of our adversaries that Nigeria is a failed state.

Nigeria can and must be a success state. In any case, Nigeria was once a success state. That was when teachers were well-motivated; school enrolment was progressively on the increase, when school curriculum met the global standard. The president and the governors have the historic responsibility to return Nigeria back to the path of development to be driven by the educated workforce nurtured by well-motivated teachers.

NIS Recruitment Tragedy or Unemployment Tsunami[*]

It is remarkable, that the Federal Government had instituted a probe into the circumstances which led to the death of scores of applicants nationwide during the recent recruitment of Nigeria Immigration Service (NIS). While this probe-panel demonstrates the sensitivity of Yar'Adua administration to get to the root cause of avoidable death of employment seekers, the latest tragedy calls for more than just another panel beating via probe. The scandalous human wastage akin to similar daily "accidents" on our "roads" occurred in Abia, Kwara, Enugu, Anambra, Edo and Bauchi states among others. When tragedies get cumulative and widespread, as the latest, then they are no more "accidents" or flash that would ebb with time. They might very well be incidents made possible by official disdain for labour and employment issues in general. The gender dimension of the sordid labour abuse also came to the fore with two of the dead reportedly being pregnant female applicants.

What the nation needs urgently is a far reaching new labour market policy that will put an end to this serial primitive recruitment exercise which, leaves in its trail despair, tears and dead bodies rather than living applicants.

The nation has witnessed much of distortions in the labour market in recent time. It is not clear why a nation that is signatory to relevant ILO standards with respect to Decent Work would be so vulnerable to avoidable labour disaster 200 years the world terminated the horrendous slave market.

---

[*] *The Daily Trust*, 21ˢᵗ July 2008

94

Three critical labour market issues flow from the recent immigration/prison service recruitment tragedy. They are worsening unemployment situation, absence of labour exchange centre and official lack of appreciation that labour market functions differently from any other factor market. The three can be summed up as absence of decent employment agenda by Nigeria's governments at all levels in general. All the issues are also governance issues which task the responsibilities and sensitivities of the Federal as well as State Governments of the Federation.

NIS has placements for 3,000 new employees but at the last count, as many as 195,000 applicants, reportedly turned up nation-wide for the ill-fated interview which never took place for some. Nothing dramatises Nigeria's unemployment crisis than the painful fact that so many applicants were called for such scandalously limited opportunities! The official unemployment rate is said to be 16%. But NIS' dramatized labour demand and supply statistics clearly belie this official unemployment rate according to Bureau of Statistics. What Nigeria has at hand is disaster as far as unemployment is concerned. The custom service has just announced similar recruitment exercise. The point cannot be over-exaggerated that as many as those that turned up for immigration would still troop out for the Custom service. If the absorptive capacity of the Federal departments such as Customs and immigration is so limited, we can then imagine the limitations of the private sector already constrained by factory closures, under capacity utilization, absence of power and high cost of production.

Nigeria is actually in a state of emergency as far as unemployment, underemployment and idle capacity are concerned. What the government needs is to officially recognize this grim reality and roll out (not just declare) emergency measures. America after the Second World War was not confronted with this scale and dimension of unemployment; school leavers of different grades before President Roosevelt declared a new deal, the bedrock of which was affirmative commitment to full employment at all costs including paying people to dig and fill same holes.

Yar'Adua administration should urgently break the jinx of the painful paradox of a country with so much to be done in all sectors, with so much resource endowment and yet inexplicably saddled with such huge idle hands. Today school graduates have all the degrees, Bsc, BA, MSc, MA, PhD but they lack the singular degree to terminate income poverty, which is JOB.

NIS deaths did not occur due to any so-called rigorous exercise as demanded by the requirements of the services. On the contrary what we witnessed was unemployment tsunami in which many hands are desperately seeking ways out of income poverty that employment offers through miserable narrow outlets. Added to this was the rather clumsy ill-informed arrangement of the NIS bureaucracy, the result of which was mass death than real interview for living applicants as known in civilized world of work. The event of the last week is a rude awakening for the administration to create jobs, jobs and jobs (in-that-order). Promotion of mass employment opportunities is fundamental for Nigeria's economic recovery while conversely idle capacity pushes the country into under- development. We cannot be part of the 20 leading economies with idle school leavers and army of under-employed such as *okada* riders whose value addition is suspect. The first challenge for Nigeria is to place employment at the heart of economic and social policies. Each of the 7-point agenda has the potential of mass job creation such that many jobs should be chasing many seekers. But that is if somebody, somewhere, realises that employment and job creation as well as job retention are both the means and ends of the agenda for sustainable development. We must pursue job-led growth and *not* jobless growth.

When jobs are created (as they must urgently be mass created), there must be profound appreciation that labour market is not another capital market, with all the attendant frenzy of bearishness and bullishness. Job seekers are not stocks to be thrown up for grabs. Since humanity rightly banished slave trade (with prescribed punishment for slave traders!), Labour is no more a commodity to be bought at a bazaar as NIS "recruitment" centres exhibited. Labour markets "are socially embedded" for those that care. Labour markets harness human energies. They rely on human motivations, care, understanding, dignity and above all fairness. We have witnessed so much labour market indignities ranging from pensioners dying on "verification" exercise to the latest murder via recruitment exercise. Somebody must halt the recent obscene recruitment exercises in which many are called to be humiliated for limited opportunities and put in place an informed arrangement with more sensitive citizen-based interviews that would indicate the applicants are needed and valued. Pregnant women have the right to seek for employment. But our gender sensitivity is put to test when we return their dead bodies rather than offering them jobs alive. Nigeria is already notorious for high maternal mortality rate due to shameless deficit of Medicare and irresponsibility of health administrators in general. We kindly dare not add to the untimely death of pregnant women through dubious recruitment exercise. Nigeria needs functional labour exchange market through which the unemployed should register and from which employing agencies can draw on in a systematic, fair, dignified and rewarding manner. The challenge is to formulate a functional labour market policy which is currently not in place and sadly not in discourse. Granted that those that fell short of coping with the rigorous exercise were truly "unfit", what does it then say about the depravations of the unemployed in the face of challenges of income survival?

Our neo-liberal mindset must give way to social compassion that must lead to introduction of unemployment benefits for the unemployed within the context of social protectionism until they get jobs. All said all persons responsible for last week recruitment tragedy should be identified and appropriately sanctioned.

Pay Cut or Pay Equity?*

"A just wage for the worker is the ultimate test of whether any economic system is functioning justly"- *Pope John Paul II*

The move by President Musa Yar'Adua to reduce the probative compensation of political\office holders as part of some of the measures to cope with the challenges of current economic crisis has further brought to the fore crisis of compensation in Nigeria.

The President's letter to the Revenue Mobilization, Allocation and Fiscal Commission underscores governance sensitivity move comparable to emerging sensitive best practices by serious statesmen in the wake of current global recession.

Political office holders in Cote de Ivoire, a non-oil producing nation, slashed their pay in the wake of rising oil prices. One of the first bold recovery measures by President Obama of United States of America (USA) was to put a lid on upward review of the pay of White House staff arguing that Washington's remuneration could not be business as usual while impoverished Americans are tasked with belt tightening measures. At home, office holders in Ogun State had reportedly voluntarily parted with 12.5% of their pay in response to dwindling revenue.

The Federal Executive Council's move therefore comes late but better late than never! The critical question begging for answer however is: Does Nigeria need wage cut or pay equity? The answer is clear: Nigeria needs pay equity defined here as massive pay cut for unjustly over paid political office holders and their private sector

---

* *Daily Trust* (Monday, February 16, 2009)

chieftains and significant upward negotiated wage review for the mass of working poor.

Let us debate the extent of the reduction of the pay of office holders. But we cannot question the rationale of a measure that is long overdue anyway. With the recent disclosure of the Commission, an insignificant number of office holders (just 700) at Federal, and state levels part with a trillion naira in annual compensation! Add unofficial sundry /self help income ventures, (not to talk of graft and outright corruption), the level of distortion of compensation structure in favour of the tiny political elite is crystal clear.

With the best of prosperity, no nation could afford to indulge political elite that has clearly not delivered basic services like public transport, water, education, health with such unjust and unfair indulgent pay. The only way the citizenry will appreciate this gesture is for the reduction to go beyond tokenism and be seen to be far reaching and drastic enough.

The new round of pay should be linked to service delivery/ performance criteria on the part of President and other political office holders. Clamp down on unnecessary over head manifested among others in assorted convoy of official vehicles and conspicuous consumptive ventures. Exhibited lifestyles such as state weddings, state burials and state sponsored ads at a time Bill Gates is the one rudely awakening us to the reality of polio menace must be discouraged and sanctioned. We do not need a World Bank loan, (concessionary interest rate or not), to fight the scourge of polio when we can just free resources rudely currently appropriated by legislators and their executive counterparts. Until there is a significant service delivery there should be total freeze on any revised pay for the political elite.

To remove inequity in the nation's reward system, government must remove similar distortion in the private sector. Executives of banks, oil companies and telecommunication among others are prohibitively paid amidst poor service delivery and absence of growth in the real sector. There has been an unfair shift in the distribution of income in favour of few enclave businesses and business owners without dubious value addition to the economy. How earth does one explain the advertised phenomenal increases in profits amidst factory closures, job-losses and pervasive income poverty?

When profits are combined with generous allowances hidden and unhidden transfers/ insider dealings, it will be seen why the tiny rich is truly getting richer (without paying taxes) while the working people are becoming working poor with over taxed miserable pay.

The recent action of the government compliments and explains the legitimacy of NLC demand. There is an inverse relationship between the unfair prohibitive reward to few countable political office holders and the acute deprivations of millions of the working people.

President Yar'Adua's sensitivity remains meaningless if the curb in indulgence of political elite is not matched with urgent upliftment of majority of the working people who live below poverty line.

Worldwide, enhancing the purchasing power of the critical mass is seen as the urgent measure to revive the economy. The thrust of Obama Stimulus Plan is to put more money in the pocket of Americans to kick start the economy. That's America that is in temporary recession compared to Nigeria that has been in crisis of demand due to income poverty over the last three decades.

Behind almost all the strikes, which have hit all the sectors of the economy in recent time, (from teachers to doctors) is the crisis of compensation and declining purchasing power.

The real threat to democratization process is the desperation of workers in the face of falling purchasing power and the attendant poverty. A hungry man will be less tolerant and less democratic.

The economy benefits from the wage adjustment for the mass of workers in several ways. The only way to grow the non oil sector is to increase the earning power of the workers to consume finished quality goods rather patronizing second hand goods on account of income poverty.

The twin policies of naira devaluation and price inflation had eroded wages and depressed workers' real wage. Price inflation has effectively led to wage cut without the obvious dictate of the employers and the government. Even in those few sectors where there has been aggressive bargaining, the monthly average earnings and minimum wage do not compensate for the loss of income as a result of price inflation.

The miserable conditions of pensioners in recent times also added a new dimension to the crisis of reward for work. Pensioners in Nigeria truly constitute the new poor whose gratuity is either denied or paid when they are already dead.

Even with the downward fall in oil revenue, Nigeria is prosperous to meet the mass need of the mass of people as distinct from the greed of the few. What we need is to replace Corruption Agenda with Development Agenda: curb the waste, motivate people for productivity, impose aggressive regime of progressive taxation, revive the real sector, fix the infrastructure, protect domestic market against smuggling and engage mass of unemployed.

Returns on work must go beyond the present "tokenism" of "palliatives". 'Palliatives" are not for workers whose commitment is needed for the dynamic economy such as Nigeria's. Motivational financial packages must transcend 'palliatives" and guarantee living conditions for the workers.

Labour As Endangered Species*

Last Friday, Nigeria joined comity of nations to mark the great international workers' day. But the official observance of the great day as a public holiday was a passing fad than an official engaging commitment and salute of the time honoured principle of dignity of labour. Whence dignity of labour in the first instance, when indeed, labour is fast receding as the most significant factor of production and value addition in Nigeria? There is a bewildering withering away of a Nigeria's working classes of 1960s, 1970s and 1980s and its replacement with mass of unemployed, unemployable multitude of lumpen as well as gatherers and hunters of all kinds of imports. The then PRP governors in 1981 were Barkin Zuwo and Rimi. Labour is truly becoming turning into endangered species!

The bane of 2005 census is the paucity of labour market statistics useful for planning and informed policy discourse. Yet, with 20 per cent officially acknowledged unemployment rate and unofficial joblessness as high as 60 per cent, Nigeria is no more a producing/working Republic. On the contrary, with massive importation of everything from tooth pick to petroleum products, palm kernel to textile, rice to automobiles/ motor cycles, ours is a cargo-container/non-value-adding economy run by smugglers for traders and rent seekers. Few surviving work-force in fringe public sector and enclave private sectors at federal and state featured at parade grounds last weekend. But the remaining days of the year are the preserves of multitude of unemployed and under employed reinforced by traders in imports and sheer beggars.

Daily Trust, Monday, May 4, 2009

The point cannot be overstated. 140 million people cannot be spoon-fed by other workers of the world producers of the world. It is simply unsustainable, betrays the promise if self-reliance at independence. Yar'Adua administration must urgently realise the wealth generation component of the 7-point agenda.

The real challenge lies in diversification. Where the economy is diversified, industrialization serves as a source of foreign exchange. It also serves as a source of employment for greater number of the population and invariably reduces income poverty.

The dispersal of industry and the emergence of new industrial centres are the most remarkable features of globalization. In the past two decades, for instance, Japan has emerged after USA as a leading industrial power in the world. There had been dispersal of industry away from Europe and America to the newly industrializing countries of South East Asia. Africa and indeed Nigeria cannot be indifferent.

The centrality of the transformational role of industry was widely shared by post-colonial states which informed the aggressive campaign of the post-colonial government on industrialization. Industrialization was part of the post-colonial development project. Colonialism had undermined the growth and development of domestic industry through a deliberate policy of import for a protected market and blatant indifference to local efforts to promote indigenous enterprises.

UNIDO (2004) shows that manufacturing industry in sub-Saharan Africa (SSA) lags behind other developing regions in almost all measures of economic development, namely income per head, industrialization and agricultural productivity. The distribution of manufacturing activity in SSA, measured by the dollar value of manufacturing value added (MVA), is highly skewed. Only ten out of 45 countries have an MVA of one billion dollars or more, while just one country, South Africa, accounts for 27.3% of the subcontinent's total MVA. The top ten producers of manufactures (equivalent to 21percent of the total number of countries) account for 45 per cent of total MVA and the top 15 (equivalent to one-third of the total number of countries) are responsible for almost half.

With the exceptions of South Africa and Mauritius, MVA per head in the 15 most industrialized countries is very low. South Africa is the only country in which manufacturing plays a major role in both domestic output and exports, while Mauritius, an island with a population of only1.2 million inhabitants, is best described as an export platform. Low levels of MVA per head reflect the underdevelopment of African manufacturing. Beyond the factors discussed UNIDO attributes the African low performance to small markets, and the failure, (with a few exceptions like Mauritius, South Africa and Lesotho), to break into export markets. The report reveals that top SSA countries ranked by share of manufacturing gross domestic product (GDP), as well as by MVA per capita, 40 out of the 48 countries (83 per cent of SSA countries for which data are available) have an MVA per capita below $250 (UNIDO 2005).

Vision 2010 had identified manufacturing and industrialization as one of the critical success factors that by year 2010 which "should contribute about 24 per cent to the GDP and should be a major employer of labour". What is the role of manufacturing in the much talked about Vision 2020? The painful truth is that Nigeria, a country of 140 million is fast becoming a non-value adding, container-economy, exporting scarce jobs, importing everything plus unemployment. We must reinvent industry and in the process reinvent workers, then, celebration of May Day and dignity of labour makes sense.

ILO at 90[*]

The recently concluded 98th Session of the International Labour Conference of the ILO assumes a special and historic significance. It marks the 90th anniversary of the Specialised Agency of the United Nations "the principal centre of authority in the international system on labour and social policy." ILO has come of age. ILO was created in 1919 by the Paris Peace Conference after the First World War. ILO is indeed associated with the moribund League of Nations, precursor of the present United Nations (UN). In large part the ILO is one of the global institutions associated with international efforts to foster global peace which it holds that it can only be sustained on social justice. The first decade of the 20th century was a period of revolutionary fervour and class struggle and battle of ideas between nascent socialism and entrenched capitalism nurtured by primitive exploitation of the working people. ILO was created exactly two years after the great Bolshevik communist revolution led by Lenin against the despotic Tsarist Russia. Ideologically speaking therefore the organization was established to curb the spectre of communism through globalization of minimum labour standards. The objective was to moderate the hitherto primitive accumulation of capital which pushed labour into "dangerous" and "subversive" ideas of revolutions.

The principal objectives of the ILO are contained in the historic 1944 Declaration of Philadelphia. The objectives read that Labour is NOT a commodity, that freedom of association and assembly of the working people are indispensable for national progress and that poverty anywhere constitutes danger to prosperity anywhere. Even with these moderate lofty human ideals, United States of America did not join the ILO until 1934. America's ruling class in early 1990s with its avowed commitment to private property and unrestrained accumulation still maintained that ILO objectives were "socialist" and inimical to free enterprise. President Franklin Roosevelt who emerged on the ashes of the great depression led USA to join the ILO and indeed promoted the organization's ideals especially in areas of minimum wage, hours of work and social security. America's membership in turn helped in America's recovery from the depression of the 1930s.

In 1946, ILO became a Specialised Agency of the United Nations' and received in 1969, the Nobel Peace Prize.

Three organs oversee and carry out its work: the annual International Labour Conference of the entire membership; the Governing Body, elected by the Conference, which meets three times per year; and the Office, managed by the Director-General, who is elected by the Governing Body.

ILO operates through a unique system of tripartism in which representatives of workers' and employers' organisation as well as representatives of government engage as equal partners through social dialogue to address naughty issues in the world of work. Tripartism is unique to ILO and marks ILO as the most democratic of all UN agencies. Its membership is universal and operates through the instrumentalities of adopted Conventions, Recommendations, resolutions, declarations and codes of practice.

Nigeria joined the ILO from independence and has adopted most of its core conventions and recommendations in the areas of hours of work, minimum wages, right to freedom of assembly and association among others. The critical question however is to what extent has ILO membership advanced peace and social justice in the world of work in Nigeria? Military dictatorship in Nigeria violated ILO conventions and recommendations in Nigeria than civilian democratic governance. Military meddlesomeness in trade union affairs recorded serial dissolutions of NLC executives in 1988 by IBB dictatorship and dissolution of NLC, NUPENG and PENGASSAN executives by Abacha dictatorship in the 1990s and crude imposition of sole administrators.

The Governing Body of the ILO has played a critical role in cubing buses of trade union rights in Nigeria.

Nigeria has been repeatedly called upon by the ILO's Committee on Freedom of Association to release imprisoned trade unionists, end harassment of trade unions and take measures to guarantee respect for the civil liberties essential to trade union rights. The Committee underscored the persistent deterioration of trade union rights and denounced the non-respect of civil liberties in Nigeria. With proclamation of 1999 Constitution and repeal of obnoxious decrees Nigeria has undoubtedly regained its position in the world of work. The real problem however is seeming collapse of the economy, mass job losses and the withering away of the working class. Labour standards without working classes are standards in vain. Paradoxically ILO created in the heat of the crisis of the 20th century is hunted with global economic crisis at 90th anniversary. Poverty is still widely spread despite amazing global prosperity witnessed in recent times and undoubtedly poverty remains a threat to the prosperity of the few the visible club of which is G-8 group of countries. No wonder that the response to global economic crises dominated this year's conference.

NSITF: Building Social Floor for Worker[*]

Three critical labour market related bills are currently before the two chambers of national assembly for deliberations, namely Workmen Compensation Bill of 2010, the Institute of Registered Safety Professional Bill of 2010 and Workplace Safety and Health Bill 2010. Last week, the Senate Committee on Employment, Labour and Productivity under the distinguished chairmanship of Wilson Ake had a two day public hearings on the bills. Senate public hearing attracted scores of stakeholders in labour and health sectors. This week, the House of Representatives Committee on labour chaired by Honourable Ado Dogo Audu is expected to deliberate on the same bills in a related public hearing. It is refreshing that of late labour market issues capture the imaginations of our legislators. Better, late than never! Since the financial and economic meltdown, the national assembly had been hyper-active to save money and capital market from self-inflicted crises arising from greed and unbridled pursuit of profits. Conversely the national assembly has been passive when it comes to labour and human market issues even when we all know too well that it is labour and indeed human beings that often shoulder the burdens of economic and financial meltdown. In the past two years, there have been scores of legislative initiatives on how to bail out the banks and insurance companies. For instance, there were stimulus appropriations to neutralize trillions of non-performing loans in the banks. Today, protective measures are in place to safeguard banks' depositors. Energies have been dissipated to strengthen the regulatory functions of the CBN through enhanced autonomy, ensure cooperate governance of financial institutions

---

[*] *The Daily Trust* 17th May 2010

among others. These legislative measures aimed at rescuing capital and financial markets are certainly commendable. But the point cannot be overstated; there has been human and labour melt down in Nigeria with worse devastating effects than the celebrated financial and economic meltdown. With all its dramatized impact, deaths and human misery arising from labour market crisis manifestations such as mass unemployment are more grim than frustrations arising from temporary loss of incomes due to collapse of stock prices. Many workers die every day as a result of occupational health and safety hazards. Equity therefore demands that our legislators must be active on the labour market as much, as they are active on capital and money markets.

Of special interest to me out of the three labour market bills currently before the national assembly is the Workmens Compensation Act. Often wrongly cited as Workmen Compensation Act (WCA) of 1987, WCA indeed belongs to the discredited colonial era. It is better seen as Workmen Compensation Ordinance of 1942. Subsequent amendments (1958 and 1987) to the colonial piece of legislation had not in any way obliterated its obsolescence and complete irrelevance to modern industrial needs of working men and women. The notorious legislation passed at the height of Victorian colonial oppression and exploitation, is gender blind as it only envisaged male workers (Workmen) and not female employees (Working people in general). The colonial law was designed to compensate for injury at work. Broadly, the law provides for four types of benefits, namely permanent partial incapacity, permanent total incapacity, temporary incapacity and fatal accident cases involving deaths from injuries at work. Sixty years after, this legislation has not saved nor compensated for Nigerian workers who suffered daily injuries at work. Workmen Compensation Act cannot be reformed. It must be repealed and replaced with the newly proposed all inclusive Employees Compensation Act of 2010.

The bane of WCA is that claims under it depend on miserable annual pays of the affected worker (for a long time pegged at maximum of ₦1600). 42 months pay for dependants in cases of deaths and 54 months pay in case of total incapacitation of an injured worker only made negligence of health and safety standards attractive to employers especially in the private sector. We must make accidents at work expensive through legislation. In 2004 for instance, the nation was rudely woken up to the tragedy of safety disregard at work place when a fire out break at a Rubber plant in Ikorodu, Lagos state killed as many as thirty workers. Only miserable amount of money could be paid under the obsolete WCA to compensate for these singular industrial murders such that it took mass actions of NLC to get justice for the workers' dependents. Another major shortcoming of the old WCA is its legalism. The burden of proof of claims is on poor workers. In the end employers with ways and means for sustained litigations are the beneficiaries. The national assembly must repeal this old law and pass the newly proposed Employees Compensation Act (ECA). The new Act envisages a contributory scheme funded with 1 per cent contribution of employees' monthly pay by employers. This scheme allows for sustainable pool of fund to compensate an injured employee. For the new scheme to work there must be a regulatory agency to manage it. The new ECA must be taken off the private insurance companies who profit under the old WCA with little benefits for the employees. In this respect the best institution well positioned to run the ECA is Nigeria Social Insurance Trust Fund (NSITF) Born from the ashes of the defunct National Provident Fund (NPF), NSITF had traversed a road of relative successes in social insurance industry. There is certainly a considerable room for improvement in terms of benefits administration, but the NSITF is relatively better positioned to make a difference for injured working people.

Minimum Wage, Minimum Delay[*]

President Goodluck Jonathan must urgently add his presidential weight and push for a speedy legislation on a new minimum wage for Nigerian workers by the national assembly.

On July 14th 2009, the late President Musa Yar'Adua represented by the Secretary to the Government of Federation, Alhaji Mahmud Yayale Ahmed inaugurated a tripartite Presidential Committee on National Minimum Wage headed by retired Chief Justice of the Federation, Hon Justice S. M. A. Belgore, GCON. The inauguration was in response to a year-long agitation for a new minimum wage by Nigeria Labour Congress (NLC). The terms of reference of the Committee included consultation with all stakeholders on the issue of minimum wage, consideration of a new minimum wage in the context of the dynamics of national economy and a proposal for a realistic and practical minimum wage for the government. The tripartite Committee made up of representatives of Federal and state governments, organized private sector, small and medium enterprises and trade unions, namely NLC and TUC deliberated extensively for one year. The Committee examined the relevant economic indices offered by Ministry of Finance, Nigeria Institute for Social and Economic Research (NISER), CBN, relevant laws and Conventions of the International Labour Organization (ILO). At the end of its deliberations, the Committee recommended among others, a new minimum wage of ₦18,000 per month for a Nigerian worker. This figure was the negotiated outcome. The proposal of the NLC was actually ₦52,000. This recommendation was forwarded to the

---

[*] *The Daily Trust*, 30th August 2010

111

Secretary of the Federation by the Chairman of the Committee, retired Justice Belgore at a televised and generally reported historic ceremony on the 1st of July. Significantly too, (thanks to the acknowledged passion and commitment of the Chairman to a new deal for the workers!), the Committee report was accompanied by a draft new National Minimum Wage Bill of 2010 for onward transmission to the National Assembly. This unprecedented innovation in presidential committee's service delivery is expected to minimise the time loss in the process of realisation of the new minimum wage as well as expedite the process of signing the law by the President. However since then, the official voice on the piece of legislation meant to address the worsening crisis of compensation in the labour market is muted. In fact there has been a loud silence on the new minimum wage. It is time President Jonathan actively pushed a long overdue new legislation through and fulfilled his pledge to workers' welfare at the 2010 May Day a reality.

The point cannot be overstated. The objective of minimum wage is to protect the lowest wage earners and guarantee the workers a decent standard of living. Minimum wage is a labour market instrument that offers a social floor bellow which no worker falls. The principle of minimum wage as an instrument against income poverty is so clear such that historically minimum wage was never linked to workers' productivity as such. What counted was whether a worker and his/her family of a wife and four children can live on the minimum wage on offer. Some have argued that given the unemployment rate and large number of workers in informal sector, minimum wage benefits relatively few employed workers. This line of reasoning ignores the fact that minimum wage paid to a worker goes to sustain the army of unemployed any way, the ever extending family members and impacts positively on the informal economy as a bench mark. Thus minimum wage is a win-win formula against compensation crisis in general. We are legitimately pained with the stories of millions of Naira allegedly monthly paid to the legislators. Yet nobody seems worried nor alarmed that the subsisting prevailing minimum wage Act passed in 2000 offers a worker just a peanut minimum wage of ₦5,500 month. At the exchange rate of ₦150 to a dollar, a Nigerian worker earns less than $40 a month which in real teams is less than ₦125($150) a Nigerian worker earned as minimum wage in 1981. As we can see that there is an inverse relationship between the earnings of a few privileged legislators and the miserable pay of the army of working people. Minimum wage raised will definitely be a worthy instrument to address the sickening wage apartheid in Nigerian economy. There is no reason whatsoever why the promulgation of the new minimum wage Act should be delayed a day longer. The negotiation process that led to the new ₦18,000 was all inclusive enough involving all labour market actors. Thus the challenge is implementation not renegotiation. With respect to the new minimum wage, the federal government must show the same will power that made speedy appropriation of supplementary budget of ₦87 billion for INEC possible and make provision for the new negotiated rate possible in 2011 budget for the public sector workers. Also the government must direct the private sector employers to negotiate with their workers with a view of implementing the new minimum wage. The real governance issue today after the electoral reform is crisis of compensation engendered by the existing miserable pay of the working people. If the latter is not addressed urgently, it poses a real danger to the electoral reform: a poorly paid worker can hardly be a happy voter. With trillion naira annual budgets, there is certainly enough for the many only if minimise the greed of the few.

How Productive Is Nigeria?*

Yours truly was a privileged Guest Speaker at this year's 11th National Productivity Day (NPD)/Conferment of National Productivity Order of Merit (NPOM) Award. I bear witness that considerable work needs to be done on national productivity. No better time to raise the noise level of the production crisis than now; on the eve of national elections. Assuming these elections are all about the real issues; not petty zoning, religions or regions! Simply put: Nigeria is no longer a productive nation. On the contrary, we consume what we do not produce; export what we should produce in turn to import same products with tears. Productivity is an input/output relationship. Please let us now address critical issues of electricity, policy environment, education and technology to raise the nation's output. However there are even little critical success factors within our reach. The most precious input factor in productivity is time and time management. We parade highest number of public holidays on earth. Some of these holidays legitimize idleness rather than promoting decent work with respect to rest. How on earth do you declare a free working day to "mark" Democracy Day, a day arbitrarily chosen by one man in office that could even fall on a Monday? Why would children not be in schools on a Monday in the name of democracy? To deepen and defend democracy, we must work and work, read and read, not just idle away. Anti-democratic forces are at work only when we are asleep and slumber in ignorance. Nigeria works 8 hrs, 5 days a week. But on average, other 19 countries in our preferred club of 20 most developed countries, (come the magic 2020!) work longer hours, 6 days a week. Out of 365

---

* *Daily Trust*, 25th October 2010

days in a year, Nigeria is at rest for some 120 days. Out of the official eight hours, we resume unofficially at 10 am, set to do some unofficial school (children) runs by noon, only to unofficially close shops at 3pm ostensibly to beat the traffic.

We must dispute the general shock therapy approach of the Mr. Oronsaye Head of Service to civil service reforms in general. But wholeheartedly I hail his recent move and audacity to lock out scores of late comer-civil servants in the office of the Head of Civil Service of the Federation (OHCSF). We pay so much lip-service to timing and service delivery in this country. At the weekend, President Jonathan Goodluck in a Town Hall meeting in Bayelsa, mid-way belatedly remembered he ought to have been at a function by 10 am. And that was 11:30am after which he was on and on muddling through marking time! With such televised Presidential time consciousness mindset/lip service, any further evidence, why corporate airlines would delay flights whimsically with stale apologies to match? Nigeria is the only country you wait 3 to 4 hrs to catch a 45 minute flight!! It simply does not add up in costs and efficiency. Nelson Mandela once observed: "South Africans have no concept of time and this is why we can't solve poverty and social problems... By this stage we should have overcome being late all the time." Mandela's admonition is even more relevant for Nigeria at 50. In fullest of time at least South Africa had counted national votes in quick successions. In fullest of time, South Africa hosted the world cup. In fullest of time mismanagement, in Ekiti state, after three years and half, the real governor, ACN's Kayode Fayemi, just replaced an impostor PDP's Segun Oni. "Gain Time, Gain Life," goes the old received wisdom. The current debate about the crisis of electoral reform is all about timelines. Yet we had four years to have reconstituted INEC, funded it and made relevant law amendments. We have lost an hour in the morning, now we are spending all day hunting for it. Conceived in early 1990s, Vision 2010 had eluded us. Time and timing were central to the messages of all our prophets. Prophet Muhammad (peace be upon him) says in one Hadith: "There are two things that people are not aware of how important they are: health and time." For Jesus Christ "Everything He did was timed to perfection; the Scripture says that He came in the "fullness of time" – that is, at the perfect time. In 1998, we signed on MDGs for 2015. Are we meeting the eight goals before then or on time? Time management is a function of development/productivity agenda. Sadly productivity agenda is missing in Nigeria. Almost by route every Nigerian knows our position on the International Corruption Index. But pray what is our ranking in Global Productivity/Development index? Nigeria at 50 thrives on a notorious false economic idea, namely corruption/anti-corruption economics. We even featured "looted funds" in 2001 and 2002 national budgets. Remember Abacha's loot. Again, reportedly re-looted. We either pretend to be fighting corruption or corruption frontally fights us daily: from the rot of power sector to the mess of custom, from allegations in the national assembly to the racket of the sports commission/FIFA, from the banking halls robbery to the police road check points extortion. But all this hype notwithstanding, Corruption/anti-corruption economics is a false economics. If the aim is to reduce maternity/infant mortality rates, why on earth diverting insufficient health budgets for a legislative retreat in Ghana? There is absence of development agenda precisely because there is no productivity agenda. We can definitely make do with leaders of proven integrity as it was in the First and Second Republics. However, honest leaders with integrity without national productivity/development agenda will only end up preside over corruption and indeed ruination of a nation. Tanzanian Julius Nyerere was undoubtedly the most respected leaders ever produced Africa. Yet with simplicity and modest means, he left a legacy of a corrupt and poor country. So much then for integrity without productivity agenda! Nyerere confessed that he indeed failed, because he lacked development/productivity agenda. Conversely President Suharto of Indonesia did not parade integrity credentials as such. But he had a development/ productivity agenda that made Indonesia a more prosperous economy than Nyerere's Tanzania. Indonesia's GDP in 2008 (932.1 billion dollars) was thrice that of Tanzania's GDP. Despite our pretentions at fighting corruption, Nigeria's economic performance shamelessly trails well behind Indonesia.

The challenge lies in stimulating institutional productivity, not parroting from the roof tops; corruption and anti-corruption without productivity/development agenda.

10th NLC Delegates Conference[*]

I bear testimony that the just concluded 8th Delegates' conference of NLC has a lot to offer Nigerian polity in democratic transition. The conference took place from 1st to 3rd of March at *ThisDay* Dome, Abuja. The conference was as political (with 1,993 delegates/ voters for 16 contestants into about 8 elective offices) as it was also industrial (dealing with sundry issues of world of work, namely employment, wages, industry, unionization, etc.). Each delegates' conference of NLC is an equivalent (so to describe) of proclamation of a nation's new constitution in a democratic administration. 10th delegates' conference of NLC thus ushers in 10th labour's democratically elected administration or "republic". It is self-evident then that Nigeria's labour movement is long-dated in democratic process and experience than Nigerian Republic itself. This may not be surprising; the first independent and democratic union, Civil Service Union, was formed as early as 1912. Unofficially recognized unions started much more earlier in early 19th century challenging the authoritarian rule of British imperialism. Nigeria got independence in 1960. Nigeria is on the threshold of ushering in the 6th democratically elected administration. Labour movement shared together with Nigeria ill-fated history of unwanted military meddlesomeness. Of the 10th Delegates' conferences, three were special confabs. 'Special' to the extent that, they were fall-outs of military disruption of independent and autonomous democratic union process; 1977/78 (Murtala/Obasanjo military regime), 1988 (IBB regime) and 1999 (Abdulsalami regime), following Abacha's dissolution of the NLC executive in 1994. NLC cumulatively could be said to have been

---

* 7th March, 2011

suffocated under the heel of military administrators for 10 years (the highest being under Abacha dictatorship). Nigeria, however had a longer spell of military misrule spanning over two decades. Against this background of shared history of military dictatorship with the country as a whole, NLC 10th delegates' conference assumes a special importance. The successful conclusion of NLC 10th conference raises, once again, greater hope of democratic process in Nigeria and indeed Africa as a whole. Nigeria and (indeed Africa) has produced strong institutions. One of these institutions is Nigeria Labour Congress (NLC). The 2011 concluded 10th conference was historic and remarkable given that it was independently successfully and peacefully organised by the NLC and its 39 affiliate unions. We must salute the comrades for putting an end to the myth that civil society cannot organise its affairs unless it is flogged to do so by some big-brother government and petty dictators.

Worthy of mention are the proceedings of this historic conference. The address by NLC President, Comrade Abdulwaheed Ibrahim Omar under the conference theme: *"Building A New Nigeria; The Role of the Working Class Towards National Transformation"* set the tone for the conference. Labour issues that featured at the conference, included; minimum wage, pensions, decent work agenda, internal capacity development, job-creation as well as poverty eradication strategy and economy. In keeping with its theme conference demonstrated remarkable concerns for larger national and global issues that included naira value, globalisation, vision 2020, collapse and revival of industries, role of state in development process, revival of social sector (education and health) and the wave of democratization process in Arab countries. The first NLC conference that produced the founding President Comrade Hassan Sunmonu held in 1978 following the controversial restructuring of trade union movement during Murtala/Obasanjo military dictatorship. Almost four decades after, Nigerian workers have consistently reaffirmed their abiding faith in trade union democratic process notwithstanding the intolerable obstacles put on their way. This democratic commitment has produced six democratically elected workers' Presidents: namely Hassan Sunmonu (1979-1984),

(Ali Chiroma (1984-1988), Paschal Bafyau (1988-1993), Adams Oshiomhole (1999-2007) and the newly re-elected President Omar Abdulwaheed. The events in Arab countries have provoked a debate of plausibility of revolution in Africa and indeed in Nigeria. It depends on what we conceive as revolution. If revolution is about getting rid of military dictators, let it be said that the Arabs are just waking up from their unacceptable slumber to learn from the long dated struggle of Nigerians and Nigerian workers in particular for democracy. At the arrow head of this revolution is NLC that has stood up over the years for democracy and against regime and policy dictatorships that have helped Nigeria not to witness the likes of Mubaracks, Ben Alis, Robert Mugabes, Idi Amins and Ghadafis with all their attendant governance tragedies. Nigerian workers in NLC have always raised democratic flag which reads that: *workers shall elect their leaders!* With this singular democratic resolve as NLC did we can put paid to election rigging in April as Professor Attahiru Jega INEC chairman and special guest to the NCL conference rightly advocated. Interestingly (as if by design), NLC conferences serve as precursors of national elections in recent times. 8th NLC confab took place in February 2003 just before the controversial carry go-national elections. The 2007 Congress confab took place just before the most flawed 2007 national polls held. What promise does 10th NLC free and fair issue- based conference have for the 2011 April polls? Democracy is all about constitutionalism spelling out the rules of entry and exit for elected officers. With all the temptations of attachment to a winning team NLC delegates drawn from 39 industrial union affiliates kept faith with the rules of exit that confer 4-year tenure to elected council. The NLC transition was totally free of the unhelpful crisis of confidence that hunted OBJ discredited notorious third term diatribe. The success of NLC conference lies in the unity of purpose of the comrades in ensuring decent jobs for Nigerian workers and commitment to re-fix and propel Nigeria and Africa on the path of development and progress. It is this clear bigger picture that eludes some Nigeria's political elite that in turn makes them carry on irresponsibly. The dastard denotation of explosives that callously killed some people at PDP rally in Suleja was a direct opposite of comradeship with contestation at the NLC conference.

In fact a whole day (Tuesday) was devoted to debate on scores of motions and resolutions on labour and national economy, globalization, security of lives and property, labour and petroleum supply and distribution, governance crisis, labour and education reforms, trade union ethics and morality, labour and democracy and civil society as well as labour and international issues. The NLC conference was witnessed by scores of international labour movements from Ghana, Canada, Italy, OATUU. The strength of NLC confab was that it was run on *issue, issues and issues* and not persons and personage that currently weigh down Nigerian politics hostage. Comrade Governor Adams Oshiomhole, Olusegun Mimiko and Sylva witnessed the opening session. Governor Oshiomhole two-term President of NLC true to expectation pledged commitment to pay the new minimum wage urging other governors to respect the national minimum wage law. When elections are based on issues, there is hardly loser. In fact all the delegates at NLC conference were winners in the sense that while all candidates did not win, all unions had their motions and resolutions incorporated into 4-year agenda of the new NLC leadership. The lesson for politicians is that campaign must refocus on issues. Issues cannot be rigged!

Wanted - Emergency on Job Creation*

Observers of the colourful May Day mass parade at Abuja Eagle Square yesterday jointly organized by mega labour centre, Nigeria Labour Congress (NLC) and Trade Union Congress (TUC) must have been impressed undoubtedly by the large turnout of organized workers in their respective industrial unions marking 2011 workers' day. Kudos to the leadership of the NLC led by Comrade Abdulwahed Omar in particular for such remarkable level of organization for a May Day parade which had the Vice President Sambo Namadi representing President Goodluck Jonathan in attendance as well as scores of ministers and fraternal national and international federations that included OATUU, represented by its General Secretary, Comrade Hassan Sunmonu. Precisely because yours sincerely is involved, I bear witness that 33-year old NLC is a tested labour federation that has over the decades been organizing (and not just agonizing!) in defence of the interest of the country's working people. Yet as massive as the workers' turn-out was, with an urgent frontal attack on mass unemployment through job creation, Eagle Square could even witness and accommodate more workers in subsequent May Days if we combat the existing level of mass unemployment. Ordinarily, a positive relationship exists between economic growth and job creation. As Comrade Omar's address indicated, in recent times Nigerian economic growth averages some impressive rate of between 6 and 7 per cent annually. But this growth has not led to real development in terms of jobs creation. On the contrary, unemployment and poverty are the twin visible features of

---

* May 2, 2011

122

Nigeria's economy. NLC is right to seek for a "balanced and inclusive growth" that must lead to mass job creation.

We must revisit the assumption that makes growth as end when it should be the means to job creation and poverty eradication. Annual Budget details had it GDP grew by 6 %, in the last decade. Sectorial details were no less salutary; oil and gas, telecommunication, agriculture sectors reportedly grew by between 8 and 10%. Over the years, fiscal operations recorded improvement given that internally generated revenue and external reserves substantially increased. We even had excess crude accounts and now Sovereign Wealth Fund! Good! All these growth indicators more than anything else, make the current high level of unemployment of willing hands simply inexplicable. Indeed positive economic growth indicators make mass recruitment (not mass unemployment) logical, tenable and fair in a developing economy like ours. This is what received economic wisdom teaches; economic growth must translate to expanded employment and prosperity for the citizens. We must reject the neo-liberal policies that celebrate "jobless growth". Market reformers and their institutional promoters such as the World Bank had long sold a miserable good-for-nothing image of public employment in sub-Saharan Africa. The market-place cliché is familiar; "over-staffed, under-paid and unproductive public sector". The peripatetic picture is seemingly clearly enough such that no data or explanation is offered. The policy implication is also self-evident; mass lay-offs. It is a sad commentary that this flawed assumption and its suspect policy-hang-over are finding expression in our labour market policy. *Mass unemployment and huge idle human capacity are even more expensive to the society both in the short and long terms as we have seen with the latest post election violence fuelled by idle capacity willing to unleash terror.* We may save on salaries of retrenched teachers, nurses and doctors and the police but society remains permanently hunted by the cost of such savings to public education, public health and public security respectively. There are costs, there are COSTS. The choice is certainly ours. We commendably have fashioned out a vision, expectedly to transform the political and social-economic sphere of Nigeria by 2020. The challenges Vision 2020 poses are enormous. Translating these challenges to reality rests on sound labour market policies. Nigeria must reaffirm it commitment to full employment. There are many jobs to be done, namely provision of water, health services, building of roads, housing, poverty alleviation, information, education, tax-collection and good governance in general. All these beg for more and more hands and not less. While crude oil or solid minerals are non-renewable resources, with appropriate policy-mix, labour is inexhaustibly renewable. Throwaway labour-force represents potential output denied to the economy, it's value-crudely subtracted – not added. To appreciate the problem of unemployment and joblessness we should consider the plight of the unemployed at least for once. Perhaps we may for once consider the plight of that person without job. If he or she is the breadwinner, it is clear then that the family support collapses. Food may be difficult to get to feed the children with all the implications for malnutrition. Some kids may be withdrawn from school on account of non-payment of school fees while Easter and Sallah cloth will necessarily elude them. Pray the family is not sick either. Since the breadwinner cannot meet expectation, depression logically replaces love within the household. The options before the unemployed in a society without social security like Nigeria are therefore better imagined. It's time we opted for Labour market as well industrial policies that see employment as the means and end of development. It is commendable that the theme of this year's May Day is Job Creation and Peoples' Welfare. I agree with NLC that unemployment remains one of the greatest challenges facing our nation. Federal Government has set up a committee on Job creation and has recently held a one-day Job Summit. Several State Governments have also initiated some programmes of Job Creation, but they all constitute a drop in the sea of head counts of the unemployed.

The real challenge is the urgent need to revive the closed factories and import substitute the mass goods and services that Nigeria currently imports. *Every imported good to Nigeria means imported unemployment and exported employment while every locally produced good means job creation and job retention in Nigeria.* Happy May Day!

Understanding the New Employee Compensation Act (ECA)*

Undoubtedly mass employment is the key out of poverty. With as much as 50 per cent unemployment in Nigeria, Nigeria certainly must create *jobs, jobs and jobs.* However, as desirable mass jobs are, not all forms of employment guarantee an escape from poverty. Not all jobs create rewarding sustainable wealth either. Some jobs are not well paid for. Many jobs are indeed criminally poorly rewarded by callous and exploitative employers. Indeed in countries like Nigeria, we have millions of "new working poor people" defined here as working people who remain poor notwithstanding the fact that they are working. Their take home pay can hardly take them home talk less of feeding their dependants at home. Hence, workers through their trade unions relentless demand for what ILO rightly identifies as Decent jobs (not just any jobs). Decent jobs are anchored on minimum wage or minimum social pay floor below which a worker falls. Decent jobs are jobs that end with gratuities. Decent jobs are jobs that must be pensionable jobs. To this extent we must commend the minimum wage Act of March 2011 signed by President Goodluck Jonathan. We must also hail the enactment of Pension Act of 2004 signed into law President Olusegun Obasanjo. Less than a decade the Pension Act under the dynamic leadership of Muhammad K Ahmad, Director General of National Pension Commission (PENCOM) had pooled some trillions of naira for working men and women after retirement at work.

---

* August 1, 2011

Yet after we have made jobs pensionable and pay gratuities at exit points, there are also precarious jobs associated with risks and hazards! Accidents and injuries characterise many forms of employment; especially in construction, textiles, chemicals, iron and steel industry, mines, etc. Every year, some two million men and women lose their lives through accidents and diseases linked to their work. In addition, workers suffer 270 million occupational accidents and 160 million occupational diseases each year. Precisely because of risks and hazards associated with works in general, some people have rightly observed that many working people are really not living but are actually dying *"by instalment"*!

The importance of health and safety at work cannot be overstated. Failure of many governments to enforce health and safety standards means that efforts to improve working conditions in one country can be undermined by the flight of production to countries where workplace safety is ignored. *All labour market actors and observers must support any efficient legislation and laws aimed at compensating workers for any occupational hazard/accident at work.* Hence the need for protective/compensation laws to prevent and compensate for injuries at work. Prevention of course will always be better than cure through compensation. However, with the best of prevention, accidents and injuries are inevitable at work. Beyond the new minimum wage, the Pension Act of 2004, another critical progressive labour market law of our time is the Employees' Compensation Act (ECA) 2010. Enacted into law on 17th December 2010 by President Goodluck Jonathan, it repeals the old and moribund Workmen Compensation Act (WCA) and aims at addressing the shortcomings of the 58-year-old WCA. Just like the minimum wage, ECA is a law that provides social protection for the working people. ECA provides for a compensatory protection floor for workers who sustain injuries and accidents in the world of work. All humans regardless of status some forms of social floor. Accident at work is not about class. With the best of prevention, there will also be accident. But when accidents happen, what kind of compensation does a worker get? ECA is a bold attempt to bring back social protection for the working people. ECA is a contributory scheme funded with 1 per cent contribution of employees' monthly pay (gross) payable by employers. The new Act allows for sustainable pool of fund for payment of compensation to employees who suffer from occupational diseases or sustain injuries arising from accident at work place or in the course of employment. The new law is designed to deliver a platform for "guaranteed and adequate compensation for all employees or their dependants for any death, injury, disease or disability arising out of or in the course of employment. Let us commend President Goodluck Jonathan for progressively signing into law both the Minimum Wage Act and the Employees' Compensation Act. We hail all the social actors, namely Federal Government, NSITF, Federal Ministry of Labour and Productivity, Nigeria Labour Congress (NLC) and Nigeria Employers Consultative Association (NECA) for ensuring the enactment of ECA 2010. Special commendation must go to the 6th Assembly under the leaderships of Dimeji Bankole and David Mark for passing the Executive bill after extensive debates last year. In particular we commend the board and management of Nigeria Social Insurance Trust Fund (NSITF) headed by the chairman of the board, Mrs. Ngozi Olejeme and Ag. Managing Director, Umar Munir Abubakar! They were all counted in standing up to defend the principle of social security. They also kept faith with the mission and vision of NSITF to provide social security and safety nets for all Nigerians. Regardless of its past shortcomings, NSITF once registered up to 4.3 million employee members and 40,000 employers. It mobilised as much as ₦36.6 billion pension fund within the 10 years period of 1994 to 2004. This served as basis for the take off of Trust fund Pension plc. However, NSITF needs to work harder in order to overcome some of the weaknesses observed in the management of the past social fund. NSITF must certainly improve on its corporate governance to face up to the challenge of the new ECA. The NSITF needs to develop a new data capturing technique for effective management and supervision of the employees compensation fund (ECF). Happily, NSITF is making the contributors to own the new compensation scheme through mass enlightenment on the implementation and administration of the ECA. All employers of labour must give effect to the implementation of the ECA by promptly paying and remitting to NSITF the 1 per cent employees' monthly pay (gross). All employees and their unions must also ensure compliance by their respective employers.

NECO - Mass Failure or Poorly Motivated Teachers?*

The National Examination Council (NECO), last Monday, released the results of the June/July Senior School Certificate Examination (SSCE). True to the abysmal standard of the last two years, the announced results showed another poor performance by candidates who sat for the examination. Interestingly news about the *Boko Haram* still occupied more space in print media than the mass failure-headline confirming the true value we assign to education! Devil is in the details of the latest mass failure; a total of 1,143, 169 candidates registered for the examination but only 244,456 candidates passed English language at credit level while 279,974 passed mathematics. Forty-three per cent of the number of candidates that sat for the examination passed at credit level in biology, just as 29.49 per cent attained the same level in physics and 36.18% in chemistry. In effect over 60 per cent failed. Registrar and Chief Executive Officer of NECO, Professor Promise Okpala, must have certainly built some immunity against shame associated against mass NECO failures. He betrayed no emotion. On the contrary he was reported to have described the results as "fair". With "fair" failure results like Okpala's we must search for another meaning of transformation agenda of President Jonathan with respect to education. Mr Okpala sounded upbeat on examination malpractices in which he claimed "only" 615,010 cases were recorded, adding that Ekiti, Rivers, Kaduna, Enugu and Nasarawa states topped the list. The populations of Equatorial Guinea and Cape Verde islands are 700,000 and 400,000

---

* September 26, 2011

129

respectively. Malpractices of populations of the size of nation-states cannot be described as "only" but miserably disastrous. The truth is that students in malpractices mess are as many of the combined students who have credits in both English and mathematics. The West African Examinations Council (WAEC) has also recorded mass failure in its May/June 2011 West African Secondary School Certificate Examination (WASSCE). Only 31 per cent of the candidates made at least five credits including English Language and Mathematics. Statistics by WAEC showed that of the 1.5 million candidates who sat for the May/June, 2011 WASCE, only 472,906 candidates obtained five credits and above including English Language and Mathematics. The most troubling is that these dismal results took place within the 100 days of President Jonathan's administration. The two Ministers of Education, namely Professor Ruqayyatu Ahmed Rufa'i, and Barrister Nyesom Wike in their media briefing on 100 hundred days of the administration kept mute on the serial mass candidates failures in examinations. If you don't accept there are problems and name the problems, how on earth do you find solutions? The recent NECO and WAEC damming results belie the official white washing about the state of our educational system. Nigeria needs new innovative thinking beyond endless retreats of bureaucrats of education ministry! The new buzz word in the Federal Ministry of Education is a 4-year strategic plan, which focuses on the following priority areas: access and equity; standard and quality assurance; strengthening the institutional management of education; teacher education and development; technical and vocational education, training and funding, partnerships and resource utilisation. All the above high sounding policy initiatives without improved results at examinations remain wasteful and diversionary. Nigeria often gets alarmed when few banks are distressed. We even declare emergency with a commendable activist CBN intervention and generous bailout funds and bail-out funds to the rescue. What is good for the few banks are even more urgent and desirable for thousands of our schools. We need an emergency in education sector! The country's education crisis has almost been defined in terms of falling quality, incoherent curriculum, examinations malpractices, poor funding, dilapidated structures and abysmally poor sector management. Very few do remember the teachers, the real drivers of education and their status. Nigeria Union of Teachers (NUT) has waged endless struggle to bring to the fore critical issues begging for attention in the country's education sector. Let us restore the status of teachers, (the working teaching women and men in both private and public schools) that under intolerable conditions are expected to build and sustain a knowledge society. It is remarkable and commendable that Universal Basic Education (UBE) is being revived. Nigeria has demonstrated significant commitment to the great task of meeting the Millennium Development goal with respect to achieving universal primary education. However all this pursuit comes to naught until we factor the conditions, quantity and quality of teachers who are expected to make the miracle of educational transformation possible. Robust curriculum design, state-of the-art new class rooms, a dozen Ministers of Education in a decade without motivated teachers mean mass failures! Time to reflect on the motivation and productivity of teachers, start with the restoration of the age long dignity of teaching profession. *"Teaching is the oldest profession that teaches all other professions"* goes a popular saying. In the past non-payment and delayed payment of teachers' salaries were unthinkable. In the past, governor would not impress anybody either that he had paid salary as "at when and due" as it is now the fashion to showcase the scorecard of present day governors. Teachers cultivated the well-acknowledged quality human capital of developmentalist Nigeria of the 1970s and 1980s. It is time we paid the teachers beyond the "minimum" or "relativities" and all those dignified words for income poverty. The worst assault against the status of teachers and education in general started in the late 80s with Structural Adjustment Programme (SAP). With cut in public spending on public education and the attendant delayed and no payment at all, the hitherto dignified status of teachers gave way to the miserable image of poor and neglected workforce. It is sad that this denigration of the status of teachers and teaching profession snow-balled into the new democratic dispensation of 1999 up to date. Bob Talbelt puts it better that *"Good teachers are costly, but bad teachers cost more!"* The NECO/ WAEC abysmal results confirm the validity of this time tested received wisdom.

Fuel Price Protest - Matters Arising*

The 8-day national strike called by both the NLC and TUC (against the prohibitive fuel price hike on the eve of the new year) reinforced by mass protests by the allies of trade unions in civil society have ebbed following the strike suspension. However 2011 national strike/mass protests raise a lot of issues, which are of profound economic, political and social importance for the country. For a nation traumatized by challenges of physical security as witnessed by last Friday serial carnage and human wastages in Kano, academic analysis proves a luxury. Yours truly is also an active participant in the subsidy debate/strike saga. Participant-observation analysis certainly tasks objectivity. But as a writer who has written on the *Crisis of Pricing Petroleum Products in Nigeria* (2001) with case studies of resistance against similar products price increases in 1988 and 2000, a fall back on written memory proves handy. First is the significance of the national strike. The strike fits into the 'overt modes of resistance'. Just like the strikes of 1988 and 2000, 2011 strike and protests were visible, truly national and global with the participation of Nigerians in Diaspora. The dimension of the strike was also officially acknowledged to be significant and remarkable with yet to be estimated human-days losses. The visibility of this singular strike, its popularity puts paid to the official argument that compares the pricing of petroleum product with telecom or aviation service. If the price of any telecom product service had risen even with higher percentages, it would not have provoked a national strike of such dimension. No product pricing could have elicited two national broadcasts by the President in quick successions if not petroleum

---

product. Indeed, with regards to petroleum pricing, we are yet to witness the 'withering away' of national strikes. On the contrary, we may be having a 'new beginning' of collective actions against arbitrary fuel price increasing, a fact that must task the creativity of policy makers beyond the dogma of deregulation.

Another important issue in the strikes is their all-inclusive nature. Nigeria is a multi ethnic and multi cultural society, in which all-inclusive issues are proving difficult to realise. No thanks to both the military and civilian ruling elite that have promoted 'prebendal system in which the pre-occupation of the political actors is ethically and regionally based competition for the spoils of office.' Exclusive ethnic and religious issues are being played up and legitimized to obscure primary inclusive issues such as accountability, good governance and transparency. Often the masses of Nigerian have been turned against each other on account of divisive issues of religion and ethnicity, while they are urged to line up behind their respective regional/ethnic elite that promote these divisions but are nonetheless united in the pursuit of self-aggrandizement and sheer looting of national resources. The recent protests just like the previous ones introduced unifying issues among the citizenry regardless of their background and persuasions. For once in recent times, the ruling elite were forced to face up to the challenges of governance of the most populous country in the continent. For once, ministers were on duty almost twenty four hours while the President walked his talk to minimize overseas trips not necessarily on account of cost but in deference to protests by angry populace at home. The President could not even attend the 100 years anniversary of the oldest tested political party in Africa; African National Congress (ANC) in South Africa. The NLC action, for once, made politicians face up to the issue of governance as opposed to their dismal indulgence in resource sharing of allowances and self-appropriation.

Another matter arising deals with the outcome of the strikes/protests. This strike just like the previous ones did not lead to reversal of price increase. However, the strike made the government return to 'power bargaining' with the people which it had hitherto rejected and paid lip-service. Of course labour has rightly insisted that 97 Naira was unilateral and not negotiated, the price reduction nonetheless reflected the gains of the strike. Beyond this qualitative achievement, is the qualitative fallout of holistic cleansing of the rot in the oil sector clause at the insistence of the NLC. The recent renewed activism of both the Executive and the legislature with respect to PIB and subsidy management is one wise out come of the strike. The decision of the trade unions to call off the strikes when government had not reversed the prices to the old price of ₦65 has rightly elicited mixed feelings just as it did in 1988 and 2000, when equally old rates on all products were not reversed except kerosene. While some hailed the outcome of the strike and protests as mature, focused and manifestation of capacity of labour and democratic dispensation to resolve conflict, there are those who saw the two outcomes as "sell-outs". This controversy underscores the ambiguous role of trade unions in the struggle for social change. Conflict and accommodation are two contradictory but inseparable aspects of industrial relations. This point is often not appreciated by both the governments and critics of unions alike. On the one hand government sees labour strikes as 'subversive' and even at a point "sell-outs" to "subsidy cabals". On the other hand critics and "emergency" activists and comrades alike who hold instrumentalist notion of trade unions hoping that every strike offers opportunity to "upturn" the system are quick to smear labour. *The truth is that unions are neither "subversive" or ""sell outs" or willing to "upturn" the system but only striving to protect the working and living conditions of their members within the system.* Rather unions are labour market parties" trying to defend their members within the system and are likely to continue to do so. The strike just like that of 1988 and 2000 clearly brought out the 'conflicting' and 'accommodating' aspects of trade union movement.

Union Makes Us Strong (1)[*]

The 10th Quadrennial National delegates' conference of our great union, National Union of Textile, Garment and Tailoring Workers (NUTGWN) commences on Wednesday 28th in Asaba, capital town of Delta state. Precisely because yours comradely is involved and informed, I bear witness that this 10th historic conference makes the statement that textile union keeps faith with the aspiration of pioneer textile workers who desired 34 years ago, strong, independent and democratic organization of workers in the Nigerian textile industry, capable of defending the rights and interests of workers at work and in the society. Textile Union is one of the 43 affiliate industrial unions under the pan-Nigerian labour centre, Nigeria Labour Congress (NLC). The 10th edition of this conference further exhibits the union's commitment to culture of internal democracy notwithstanding the current challenges facing the industry, namely factory closures, job losses, de-industrialization and general slide into underdevelopment of the country. Delegates Conferences of Textile union since 1978 have become platforms for celebrations of members-workers' struggles the following areas of Collective bargaining and improvement in living and working conditions, defence of workers' rights, Health and Safety and general working conditions, Unionizing the unorganized workers, national and global solidarity with the working peoples' struggle. Delegates' conference is about taking stock of the progress that has been recorded in these areas of union's activities in the past four years and setting agenda for the future. President Obama visited Ghana in 2009. During that visit he made his famous quote on Africa; "Africa needs strong

---

[*] March 26, 2012

institutions, not strong men." But trade union struggles in Africa had revealed that the continent needs both strong institutions and strong men and women. We need strong men and women to build strong institutions. Conversely we need strong institutions to throw up strong men and women. Therefore the two are not mutually exclusive. From our record in the past years, Textile union has shown that Africa indeed has built strong institutions with strong men and women. Since the last delegates conference using the instrumentality of collective bargaining textile unions had won wage increase wages on an annual basis. Within the period we have succeeded in improving wages by over 60%. The union is yet to attain a living wage level in country with macro economic shocks and instability, but it has made appreciable progress in the match towards living wage. Despite some of the initial reservation about Pension Reform Act 2004, textile union is one of the unions in the private sector to ensure payment of the restructured gratuity and regular commitment to the new contributory scheme. The union also negotiated increase in pension contributions beyond the statutory 7.5%, following the new Pension Reform Act 2004, after almost two year negotiations, billons of naira were paid as gratuity to members. The struggle to improve pension/gratuity arrangement is an ongoing process especially in some collapsed state textile mills through collective bargaining and industrial pressures. Textile union remains committed to a policy advocacy programme on revival of industries. Without industry there are no workers. Without workers, there cannot be no union. Over the years, we have partnered with Textile Employers, NLC Affiliates in the private sector and development partners like Bank of Industry (BOI), United Nations Industrial Development Organisation (UNIDO), Central Bank of Nigeria (CBN), Friedrich Ebert Stiftung (FES) to fight for favourable industrial policy and the protection of jobs. In 2009, textile workers and allies matched in thousands on the streets of Lagos, for re-industrialization of the country. Our effort has brought some stability to the textile industry in the last 12 months particularly with the intervention of the Bank of Industry (BOI). The highpoint was the re-opening of United Nigeria Textile Plc. Kaduna in December 2010. UNT, the largest textile mill in Africa closed in 2007. As at the last count, UNT Plc has re-employed about 1,252 workers and the group is still employing more. The policy advocacy on revival of industry has been combined with unionization drive. We have made appreciable progress in our recruitment effort as over 5000 new members were recruited in factories in Kano, Lagos and Kogi as well as informal sectors. Some progresses were made in organizing workers in the garment sector as well. We have also deepened our informal sector organizing as over 20,000 self employed tailors have joined forces with the union through their Associations across the country. The union continues to strengthen shop floor education and deepens officer development training activities. The union has kept faith with the rich and vibrant tradition of workers' education. Within the last four years over 5000 workers were trained by Education and Research Department of the union. We continue to expose our officers to local and international courses. An important aspect of education work in the last four years is in the area of HIV/AIDS. Some 105 workers were trained as Peer Educators, 62 as Mobilizing Agents (HMAs) and about 15,448 workers were reached with preventive messages. Several hundreds were counselled and tested voluntarily. As a union, we are already reaping the fruits of these efforts as some of our members now live openly with HIV/AIDS without stigma or discrimination or the fear of losing their jobs. The above modest achievements show that rather agonizing over the crisis situation in our industry, we must keep organizing. The theme of the Conference is "Transforming Nigeria through Re-industrialization, Employment and Decent Work." In a sense, conference sets to increase the noise level of (and indeed compliment) the transformation agenda of the Federal government with respect to re-industrialisation and job creation. Thousands of Delegates are drawn from the textile and garment industries across the country as well as self-employed and garment makers. Distinguished Guests include the Comrade Governor of Edo State, Comrade Adams Oshiomhole mni., host Governor, Dr. Emmanuel Uduaghan, Chairman Dangote Group, Alhaji Aliko Dangote GCON, Honourable Minister of Labour and Productivity, Chief Emeka Wogu, Honourable Minister of Information, Mr. Labaran Maku, Honourable Minister of Trade and Investment, Dr.

Olusegun Aganga and Chairpersons Senate and House Committees on Labour and Industry respectively. Other dignitaries expected at the occasion are the Chairman, Nigeria Textile Manufacturers Association, Mr. Ibrahim Iganmu and Director General, Mr. J. P. Olarewaju, captains of industry, members of the civil society and international guests. The Vice President of Nigeria, Arch. Namadi Sambo GCON is expected to declare the conference open as Special Guest of Honour. The 3-day conference features a Dinner/Award Night on Thursday March 29, 2012 in which eminent trade union activists, governors and veterans will be honoured for their contributions to the labour movement and national development. Union truly makes us strong to replace poverty with prosperity.

Union Makes Us Strong (II)*

True to its commitment to keep faith with its constitutional requirement, the 10th Quadrennial National delegates' congress of the National Union of Textile, Garment and Tailoring Workers of Nigeria (NUTGWN), affiliate union of Nigeria Labour Congress (NLC) successfully held in Asaba capital city of Delta State from 28th Wednesday to Friday 30th of March 2012. The Conference co-hosted by the former President, Reginald Augulana and yours comradely, General Secretary, was declared open by Delta State governor, represented by his deputy, Professor Amos Utuama, Deputy Governor of Kaduna State, Alhaji Mukhtar Yaro represented Governor Patrick Ibrahim Yakowa with a speech that reaffirmed commitment to efforts at resuscitating closed textile mills in Kaduna state. Honourable Minister of labour, Chief Emeka Wogu, the Registrar of Trade Unions, the Director of Trade Union services, Director General of Textile Employers Association, Senator Walid Jubril of UNTL plc, Alhaji Aliko Dangote, represented, Delta state council NLC leaders, NLC president Abdul Waheed Omar, scores of presidents and general secretaries of industrial unions witnessed the historic opening ceremony. The conference theme "Transforming Nigeria Through Re-industrialization, Employment and Decent Work" sets the tone for the official reaffirmation for revival of dead industries, growth of the real sector, job creation and defence of workers' and trade union rights. Was this an official ritual rhetoric or a renewed commitment to productive (as distinct from sharing/corruption) agenda? Time will tell if the moribund Asaba Textile mill will be reactivated as promised by the state governor in

---

* April 2, 2012

140

his speech. Notable fraternal development partner organizations that graced the occasion included Friedrich Ebert Foundation (FES) Michael Imoudu National Institute for Labour Studies (MINILS) Ilorin, Bank of Industry (BOI), National Productive Centre, National Directorate of Employment, (NDE), National Pension Commission (PENCOM), National Social Insurance Trust Fund (NSITF) as well as Trust Fund pension administrator. All the labour market/ development institutions were honoured with Partnerships awards for adding value to the work of the unions in areas of policy advocacy and industrial revival (BOI), productivity awareness (NPC), capacity building (MINILS), NSITF (employee compensation Act) and sustainable institutional support (FEF). There was a pre-conference workshop on Women participation in Trade unions in collaboration with the FEF. The union veterans were also honoured. Significantly all the past and current Presidents of NLC; Hassan Sunmonu, Ali Chiroma, Pascal Bafyau, Adams Oshiomhole and Abdulwaheed Omar were recognized for service delivery to Nigeria's working people.

True to expectation the Delegates Conference featured discussions and debates on the union struggles in the areas collective bargaining and improvement in living and working conditions, defence of workers' rights

Health and Safety and general working conditions, unionizing the unorganized, internal union democracy, national and international trade union solidarity as well as assessment of the political economy of the nation and the world. Scores of motions were intensely debated, adopted and rejected on areas of Unionization Drive, Occupational Health and Safety,

Union Education, National and International Solidarity, HIV/AIDS, plight of members in closed factories, struggle for living wage and decent work agenda in general. Students of labour studies, two perspectives emerged from the recently concluded NUTGWN congress namely; Unionism as a service and unionism as a cause. For one, it is clear that NUTGWN prides itself as an organisation concerned with the survival of the industry guided by realism. It has joined the campaign against smuggling, and wholesale trade

141

liberalization and reopening of factories closed. It has also moderated without compromising collective bargaining in the condition of crisis, factory closures and under-capacity utilization. Secondly with respect to unionism as a cause, the textile workers see themselves as a family that acts in unity to pursue common goals. NUTGTWN participated in major strikes to press home its demands. In all NLC-directed collective actions, NUTGTWN had set the standard in scope and duration. This is remarkable in a nation plagued in recent time by community clashes and even religious feuds and in which collective actions are proving difficult. Within the context of the broader labour movement, the textile workers are better equipped with an organization to promote a cause that fosters union rights and social justice. The collapse of the Leninist vision and model of 'workers' socialist society has ushered in despair in national and international trade union movements. Trade unionism has not only lost the generous material but the moral and ideological aid of the recent past. The NUTGWN conference shows that trade union movement has not accepted in any way the theory of the 'end of history' of unionism. NUTGTWN within the context of NLC is championing the struggle for the promotion and advancement of trade union rights in Nigeria.

Bjorn Beckman is a Swedish political economist who has written extensively on union power in Nigeria's textile industry. In his solidarity message to the conference, he has asked a rhetorical question; Is there no more "union power"? to which he answered in the affirmative; "Yes of course"! The high point of the conference was the election of new President, General Secretary, Deputy Presidents, Treasurer, Trustees and auditors to run the affairs of the union for the next four years. The keenly contested elections were transparently supervised by South African Thambo Shabalala of the African regional office of International Textile and Garment Workers' Federation and Nigeria's Registrar of Trade Unions. Winners and "losers" alike embraced each other making all to be winners as long as the union's struggle for better future continues. With this robust internal democracy, it is clear trade unions are not withering away even as they face new challenges to protect the gains of members and improve on them.

The NUTGTWN record also shows that trade unions perform meaningful roles within the Nigerian federation and will continue to do so in the coming years.

Pension Fraud - what about the Pensioners?*

The miserable conditions of pensioners in were hitherto discussed in terms delayed payments of benefits, poorly coordinated verification exercises and huge arrears of entitlements. It is a truism that Pensioners in Nigeria truly constitute the new non-working poor whose gratuities and terminal benefits are either denied or paid to no one even when they are already dead. Ongoing serial televised revelations of alleged pension frauds in the Federal Civil Service and Police Pension Commission in billions off naira of deferred pensioners' payments are the latest in the ugliest profiling of the pension crisis. The latest pension scam has shown that retirees' worsening plight is another fall out of the country's worsening corruption crisis. President Jonathan must urgently intervene to safe the nation's pensioners in the public sector from their existing continuous income poverty not because pensioners had not worked hard for the raining days but because few notable official criminals are looting pension funds. On-going accusations and counter accusations of bribery, plain theft and fraud between some directors of Police Pension Board and some senators, on one hand, and fraud-star words-exchange between the Senate joint committee on Establishment and Public Service and states and local governments, and Pension Reform Task Team, (PRTT), headed by AbdulRasheed Maina on the other hand over ₦2billion bribe shows that pension matters are too important and too fundamental to be left in the hands of Pension reform taskforce team and the senate committee.

---

* April 16, 2012

President Goodluck Jonathan therefore has the constitutional duty to apprehend pension theft and deepen the pension reform to ensure pensioners are adequately paid as at when due. Notwithstanding his perceived selective anti-corruption drive, President Obasanjo in 2005 offered leadership to decisively remove a Minister of Education on allegation of bribery in education sector. The late President Yar'Adua also promptly apprehended corruption in the health sector in millions of naira. President Jonathan must come out and deal decisively with the reported public Pension thefts reportedly in billions of naira, failing which the labour movement has a duty to ensure perpetual protection of pension funds through legitimate mass protests. Corruption agenda has sadly replaced development agenda in dangerous full cycle full cycle; from power sector, education sector, health sector, sports now to pension. Pension sector corruption is not just an economic crime. Theft of terminal benefits of our heroes of labour past must be seen as a treasonable crime. Taking terminal benefits of millions of pensioners, (which are far from being enough to sustain long life expectancy) amounts to burying the future of the existing workforce and mass early burials of the current pensioners.

It is unacceptable to see pension funds suspects smiling to "trials" over looted billions stashed in private bank accounts and illegal private properties laundering, while we see miserable, old, fragile and weak Pensioners being compelled to travel long distances for official 'verification' and 're-verification. Every working man and woman, including President and governors must get fatigue one day. Hence the need to prepare for the proverbial raining days by setting aside some funds that will at least meet the subsistence needs of the aged workers. With the collapse of the extended family support and traditional values of historic care and concern for the aged especially since the beginning of notorious structural adjustment, every active and young worker today can only ignore the issue of pension scheme at the instance of his/her sustenance after work. Pension is therefore a legitimate right of workers. It is a deferred payment, which both the workers and employers must set aside so that workers at old age will not be living on some charity as if they are destitute. The bane of public sector pension lies in its non-contributory character. The pension scheme is still regulated by obsolete Pensions Act of 1979. Precisely, because it is non-contributory, public servants are not required to contribute any financial sum into the schemes. Conversely it is assumed that somebody would devote some funds for the scheme which is increasingly not so. Until Public Pension Scheme is made to be contributory, it will be treated as no man's business depending on the whims and caprices of government officials. Contributory scheme is clearly more sustainable. For one, it will be free from recurring government budget crisis (or is it budget confusion?). Secondly, workers and their unions will have more interest to manage the scheme they freely contribute into when they are at work rather than living it until they are out of work and thus prevent the current outright robbery of the fund. The way we eventually resolve the existing pension crisis puts to test our real commitment to welfare of the citizenry, poverty eradication and even anti-corruption campaign. The monumental fraud in the old moribund pension system again raises the debate about the superiority of the new 2004 *contributory* pension scheme to the old *deferred benefits* scheme. Latest fraud revelations show that the old system is open to unrestrained fraudulent criminal abuses. With all the challenges, the new contributory pension system has in built check and balances with established institutions and above all distinct but complimentary functions of Pension Fund Custodians (PFC), Pension Fund Administrators (PFAs) and the regulatory agency; PenCom which are professionally run to manage funds. It is commendable that the new scheme under the regulatory agency; PENCOM managed by M. K. Ahmad in the last eight years safeguarded a trillion naira pension assets that are immune from pension marauders of the old public scheme. The challenge is for the federal government to deepen the current pension reform, strengthen the regulatory role of PENCOM and upgrade the sanctions procedure for non-compliance with the 2004 Pension Act. The pension Act contributory coverage must be made to be truly universal. President Jonathan must halt the pressures by agents of pension fund theft for a return to the old discredited non-contributory unaccountable fraud prone scheme.

Doctors' sack - end of Decent Work[*]

A casual labour observer might possibly not remember the causes of the widening rift between striking doctors under the employment of the Lagos state government and the government. But the reactions and counter reactions of both the government and the doctors have dominated public imaginations. In unprecedented public sector mass largest layoffs in the state's public service, the Lagos State government summarily dismissed the 788 doctors who participated in a three-day warning strike between April 11 and 13, 2012. Also in a similar unprecedented mass recruitment of medical doctors, the government announced mass employment of 373 doctors for immediate deployment in the public hospitals. At the last count of reactionary measures to curtail the striking doctors, the Lagos State Government has also ordered doctors sacked to vacate their official quarters. If all these measures of the Lagos government stand, we can as well say farewell to decent work agenda of the ILO ratified by Nigeria government. Decent work agenda says workers have the fundamental rights and of course duties in the world of work. The agenda hold that Labour is *not* a commodity that can be disposed of and replaced as Lagos government is doing. Indeed labour markets are socially embedded. Labour markets harness human energy. They rely on human motivations and needs, including the need for security and fairness of treatment. Decent Work Agenda puts employment at the heart of economic and social policies and development. The Agenda proposes that decent work is a productive factor, an input into a strategy for productive job creation, development and poverty

---

reduction, rather than an output alone. Governments, in cooperation with the social partners, should ensure that this right is universally accessible. It is the responsibility of all employees to make use of the opportunities offered by this agenda. Collective bargaining is a vital institution for fulfilling the objectives of labour market policies and labour market adjustment, at the enterprise level and above. The unilateral mass sack of 788 medical doctors in the Lagos State Public Service by the Lagos State government is a direct assault on Nigeria's robust labour market laws and practices that have made up the decent work agenda over the years. All labour market actors namely government, employers and trade unions should impress on Lagos State government and striking medical doctors to urgently return to social dialogue and address the demands of the doctors and the plights of agonizing patients. The demands of the doctors in particular and the medical workers in general for improved conditions of service and full implementation of the Consolidated Medical Salary Scale (CONMESS) call for social dialogue. Social terrorism that manifests in forms of shock therapy mass sack of doctors feverish eviction of doctors from their quarters, or ill-informed endless frequent strike actions on the part of the medical doctors is not a substitute for genuine social dialogue in the world of work. The impact assessment of the actions of Lagos State government so far is a total devastation of medical services of public hospitals in Lagos. The recent unfortunate development in Lagos shows that development agenda in Lagos or Nigeria as a whole is not sustainable without robust sensitive labour/human resources policies on the part of government. Lagos has recorded tremendous achievements in physical infrastructure. But the Fashola government, like some states' governments, suffers human resource management deficit as manifested in regular work stoppages and acrimonies in world of work.

Today in Lagos, we are sadly burying some patients who could have lived not because there are no hospitals, but precisely because the government that built the very hospitals lack the capacity to engage the working people namely; doctors and nurses who are expected to ensure service delivery. There are labour market institutions namely; the Industrial Arbitration Panel (IAP) and the

National Industrial Court (NIC) that should handle industrial disputes. Interestingly, the Lagos doctors' strike is already in industrial court and all parties must obey the rule of law. The striking doctors should however also appreciate that strike is not an end itself but only a means to an end that must be applied with an eye on resolution of the problem and sensitivity to the plight of the public especially poor patients who cannot afford the prohibitive bill of a private hospital service. The end in this case is the general welfare of the doctors in Lagos and service delivery to poor patients of Lagos, not the unacceptable and illegal mass sack.

ASUU - in Praise of Institution Building[*]

Academic Staff Union of Universities (ASUU) concluded its 17th delegate's conference in Abuja at the weekend. This Conference assumed a special significance with the historic commissioning of the first ever fully built national secretariat by the union. On the eve of ASUU conference Nigeria just observed another Democracy Day (29th May) as well as the 13th anniversary of uninterrupted democratic process. Often the achievements of notable "democratic" state actors capture imagination during democracy day celebrations. But what of inherently democratic organizations like trade unions and civil societies? Our assessment of the country's democratic process must go beyond the periodic controversial elections of President, legislators and governors alike and their taunted achievements. We must extend the democratic searchlight and have a critical assessment of the non-state institutions such as trade unions. Trade unions are not only loud legitimately demanding for good governance and expansion of democratic space but they are also expected to be accountable and truly representative of the workers they lead. I bear witness that ASUU like most unions, is a role model in internal democracy. With turnover of 17 Delegates' Conferences since 1978, ASUU is a union to beat in terms of biennial reaffirmation of its constitutional provisions with respect to election of its principal national officers and report of stewardship of the elected officers with respect of members' rights.

ASUU has somewhat assumed some notoriety for strikes! No thanks to lack of good governance and non-respect of freely negotiated agreements which in turn engender little options other

---

* June 4, 2012

than serial strikes! Yet all considered, when the history of education is written in Nigeria, ASUU's role in pushing for radical educational reforms through increased budgetary allocation and remunerations of for lecturers must occupy a special chapter. Ultimately we have seen through ASUU's struggle that sustainable reform in any field including education is that reforms that is driven from bellow. Today increased budget allocations to education whether at Federal or state levels must be credited to the struggle of ASUU as well as other trade unions in the education sector. ASUU has undoubtedly succeeded in putting education on the agenda of government. Special commendation must go to Professor Ukachukwu Awuzie-led ASUU for taking the union to the prestigious club of unions with their own National Secretariats. The outgoing President at the commissioning ceremony duly acknowledged the past efforts of the previous Presidents of the union to make the commissioning possible. In particular he observed that the "journey to this day started under the visionary leadership of our past president, Dr. Dipo Fashina, who with his team deemed it necessary for the union to diversify its activities into investment in areas that would enhance our assignments as academics." True to its democratic tradition, ASUU has to even debate the obvious; whether ASUU must go into investment. We were told that there was "...a school of thought in the union who felt that ASUU had no business in investing in anything like landed property or shares." Today that is all part of history as the union has worked its debates by commissioning the building and its landscaping that cost the union about five hundred million naira:

> "The complex has the following provisions: Hall of Fame; main library; research library; reference and digital library; offices for president, Librarians; administrative staff; accounts department; conference halls; and seven suites and five chalets. The rooms are all air conditioned; there are internet services, a cyber café, bookshop, two security booths and a well landscaped environment."

Yours sincerely was at the foundation laying ceremony last year. It is remarkable that ASUU beats the record time to build a secretariat, thanks to judicious management of members' funds and contributions by well wishers such as comrade Governor of Edo State who pledged and promptly redeemed N20 million for the foundation. Commendable that ASUU has worked its talk. This should be a good example for the government. ASUU has certainly produced both strong men and a strong institution. Some past Presidents of ASUU Prof. I.O. Agbede-1977-1978 Dr. B.A. Ogundimu-1979-1980; Late Dr. Mahmud M. Tukur 1980-1982; Prof. Festus Iyayi -1982-1986; Prof. Attahiru Jega-1987-1990; Prof. Biodun Jeyifo - 1990-1994; Prof. Assisi Asobie-1994-2000; Dr. Dipo Fashina-2000-2004; Dr. Abdullahi Sule-Kano -2004-2008.

Long live ASUU!

Centenary of Nigeria Labour Movement[*]

The Nigeria Civil Service Union (NCSU) headed by its National President Comrade Kiri Muhammed marked the centenary celebration of the union with a remarkable historic institution building gesture; the official commissioning of its national secretariat at prestigious area of Zone 6 on the 29th of August, 2012.

Nigeria Civil Service Union was officially recognized as a trade union in 1912 by the British colonial authorities making it the first official trade union in Nigeria. Trade unions, like any other institutions are products of their peculiar historic realities. Centenary anniversary means celebration of hundred years of continuous struggles of Nigerian workers for improved working and living conditions and forging a common organizational front to achieve set objectives. Professor Dafe Otobo (1995) a leading African author of scores of books on labour struggles identified four important events, which shaped the growth of trade union movement before the reform of mid-1970s. The events were colonialism, World War II, nationalism and the Cold War.

The significance of colonialism in the process of union formation cannot be over-emphasized. Modern employment and wage labour dated back to colonial times. Before the advent of European rule, traditional economy relied on either family or communal labour. Since there were no distinct employers in this subsistence economy, 'workers' in the modern sense and indeed trade unions were non-existent. British colonialists assaulted and

[*] *Daily Trust*, September 3, 2012

dismantled the old production order and in place erected economic system which 'became synonymous with 'collision, conflict and class struggle'. Colonialism required wage labour in public works, infrastructure construction such as railways and administration. Early trade unions thus emerged mainly in the colonial service (read; slave labour) sector, missionary schools and railways. The first generation of trade unions understandably thus included Nigeria Civil Service Union (1912), the Nigerian Union of Teachers (1931) and Nigerian Union of Railwaymen (note; no women) (1932). Unions came into existence with the main objectives of ameliorating the deplorable working conditions during the exploitative and discriminatory system that characterized British colonial rule. Since the emergence of the first generation trade unions, thousands of trade unions have been formed in Nigeria. Today, Nigeria has a system of vibrant industrial unionism as distinct from the house unions of pre-1975 era. This system means that trade unions are formed along industrial/trade lines in which every 'junior' or 'senior' worker in an industry belongs to the same trade union with the 'senior' staff belonging to senior staff associations. The unions are in turn affiliated to national labour centres, the largest, oldest and tested centre being the Nigeria Labour Congress (NLC) with as many as 40 affiliate unions and 5 million workers drawn from the public and private sectors of the economy. NLC itself is affiliated to Organization of African Trade Union Unity (OATUU) and the global union, International Trade Union Confederation (ITUC). All industrial unions are also affiliated to their respective international global unions. Recently three global unions in textile and garment, mines, electricity and petroleum sectors merged to form a mega centre-IndustriALL with 50 million workers from manufacturing sectors world wide.

Thus today the nascent trade union, NCSU (which was indeed actually inaugurated on the 19th August, 1912) had transformed into a multi-industrial, national and global labour movement thanks to the perseverance and sacrifices of Nigerian working men and women in the past 100 years.

It is therefore self-evident that labour movement is older than Nigerian Republic itself. Nigeria got Independence in 1960. Indeed the struggles of Nigerian trade unions for better working conditions laid the foundation for the struggle against British system of exploitation and oppression that led to Independence. Amalgamation of both the North and the South took place in 1914 two years after pan-Nigerian labour union had been formed. Trade unions must therefore be celebrated as the first and foremost pan-Nigerian organisations that symbolise the unity and common struggles of all Nigerians for independence and development. Trade unions preceded Nigeria army, police, parliament and even Nigerian political parties which came into existence in 1920s. Trade unions must be treated with policy sensitivity that acknowledges their developmentalist roles in colonial and contemporary Nigeria.

It is remarkable that 100 years ago, the very crisis of compensation in terms of low pay that fired the urge of workers to form a union in 1912 persists today. The centenary speech of Comrade Kiri decried the non-payment of minimum wages by some state governments as well as some Federal MDAs. If colonial exploiters denied minimum wages and were fought and defeated by the founding labour leaders like Michael Imoudu, public sector union leaders have the same legitimate right to engage state governors that choose to govern with slave labour 52 years after Independence. It is clear that from policy advocacy and mass protest intervention for good governance our trade unions are not withering away but they definitely face new challenges such as deepening internal democracy, capacity building if they must protect the gains of members and improve on more than 100 years of achievements. Abundant record shows that trade unions perform meaningful roles within the democratic system and will continue to do so in many coming years. Happy centenary anniversary comrades!

Rethinking Labour - II*

Arguably no Nigeria's Central Banker, has in recent times promoted development financing with an eye on growing the real sector and ensuring job creation like Sanusi Lamido, the CBN governor. The issues are refreshingly familiar by now; critical intervention fund for automobile, agriculture, aviation and textile among others. In the case of textile, United Nigeria textile Plc in Kaduna had since reopened and reengaged over 1500 workers on account of Bank of Industry (CBN) long term intervention fund. CBN, living up to its brief as a lender of last resort initiated a globally acknowledged timely bailout funds of some trillion naira for some five banks ($2.6 billion dollars). It is therefore a curious irony that Governor Sanusi would be the one pitched against the organised labour on the question of job retention and job creation to which both the NLC and CBN as institutions to my knowledge share common understanding.

CBN governor was reported to have called for some 50 per cent downsizing of the country work force. Investigation however reveals that the media embellished the work force alleged story more for sensational value than a serious policy discourse. True to the governor's well known position, he has been consistent in interrogating the costs of governance that include the maintenance costs of governors and legislators and other political office holders in general. But even the "correct version" of the reported work force sack story according to the CBN still raises a conceptual problem of "too many public servants" and the need for so-called "slim" and "trim" work-force.

---

* December 3, 2012

It is regrettable that labour has been condescendingly treated in our top-down/managerial perception of the economy particularly since the inception of Structural Adjustment Programme (SAP) in mid-1980s. We often engage in unhelpful binary discourse between recurrent and capital expenditure. It is almost a received wisdom that the more the capital expenditure the more development while high recurrent spending leads to stagnation and underdevelopment. May be. But in the real world of nation building, it is misleading to pitch recurrent spending against capital expenditure. A nation needs the two in equal development proportions. It is not one or the other but both if Nigeria must get out of underdevelopment. You cannot build schools without teachers nor can there be teachers without schools. Roads are built and supervised by work force while workers cannot get to work without good roads. Good governance calls for appropriate mix of both recurrent and capital expenditure. The bane of development crisis in Nigeria is that we have not been having value for public expenditure in general. In the age of deficit financing it is convenient to blame high recurrent spending for all the woes. But are we having value for the relatively small capital expenditure given the open robbery called corruption and abysmal capital flight of unimaginable proportions? I think policy makers must rethink labour and workers in general. Labour well motivated creates wealth. Labour is not just a cost item but value adding assets which we must cultivate for development. The challenge is how to make sure that marginal productivity of labour equals the wage income.

It is an open knowledge that most governments and even enterprises and managers do not know what their costs are or how to cut them. Interestingly, the "cost-saving devices" handy to most employers are retrenchment, cut in wages and cancellation of negotiated benefits among other anti-labour measures. Government as employer of labour is also guilty of these unjust measures often informed by the rule of the thumb. Labour, at all levels of analyses accounts for less than 10 per cent of cost of doing government businesses. Thus, the spectre of "cost-saving devices" must turn elsewhere; public debts and attendant prohibitive interest rates, bloated executive pay, public theft, public and private corporate fraud and endless examples of profound mismanagement and sheer corporate criminality as CBN discovered with some banks recently.

The message here is: if we must halt the unjust measures that shift the burden of the economic crisis on labour and labour alone otherwise we should expect less in terms of productivity. The motto of NLC reads: Labour Creates Wealth. This means trade unions are conscious of their responsibility to productivity beyond the trouble – making function/wage collecting-do no job function attributed to them. Every employer or investor knows that of all the factors of production human resource is the most important. Indeed the key to the success stories of countries like China, Japan, Malaysia and India is the creative manner labour has been motivated and mobilized for unprecedented growth and development. These countries lack non-renewable resources like crude oil but are nonetheless abundantly blessed with human resources in quantity and quality as in China. Successive Nigerian governments have been unable to appreciate the role of labour as a source of wealth that needs to be cultivated for development through a defined structure of incentives, training and retraining, involvement in decision making processes and organizational building and not budget balancing downsizing feverish proposals. Economic recovery will elude Nigeria until it stops treating labour at arms length.

President Woodrow Wilson of United States (1913) said 'the great struggling unknown masses of the men who are at the base of everything are the dynamic force that is lifting the levels of society. A nation is as great, and only as great, as her rank and file'. In a similar vein, Vice-President Walter Fredrick Mondale under Carter Administration (1977-1981) remarked that 'we have the most wealth of any nation because our workers have the skill to create it. We have the best products because they know how to make them. We have the most democratic system because of the values our trade unions have to sustain it'. Whence the quotable quotes of our leaders underscoring the significance of workers in nation's development?

Nigeria: in defence of Pension Assets[*]

President Goodluck Jonathan in the New Year has the responsibility to urgently call to order the Chairman of the Presidential Pension Reform Task Team (PRTT,) Adulrasheed Maina. Importantly President Goodluck Jonathan has the additional responsibility to safeguard and protect the eight-year old pension reform of 2004 which currently stands at 3.6 trillion naira.

Stakeholders including the organized labour led by NLC watch with utter dismay how Maina last year defied public summons by the Senate Joint Committee on Establishment and States and Local Governments during its recently concluded public hearing on public pension administration. Also clearly unacceptable is the way and manner the controversial chairman of what is supposed to be a short term presidential task force carries on as if the task force (meant to manage police pension fund mess and which clearly lacks any legal backing whatsoever ever!) has come to stay permanently. Presidential task force cannot and should not be another alternative pension commission in the country. There is only one regulatory pension commission and that is National Pension Commission, PenCom established by an Act of parliament in 2004.

Maina has been making ill-informed, unguarded commentaries on the accumulated pensions assets contributed through the hard earned savings of Nigerian workers in both the private and public sectors of the economy in the past eight years the Pension Reform Act of 2004 came into being. These commentaries if unchecked are capable of undermining the budding national pension fund and even subverting the entire pension market. For instance he was recently

---

[*] *Daily Trust*, January 7th, 2013

159

quoted as saying that about trillion naira pension assets already built in the pension system commendably managed by PENCOM led by M. K. Ahmad and scores of pension fund administrators, PFAs as well as pension fund custodians should be made available to the state governments for their so-called infrastructural development in clear violation of pension reform Act of 2004 and investment rules guiding pension fund in the country.

The point cannot be overstated. Pension funds assets (contributed by close to six million workers) are a contributory scheme by workers for pension after work. Nigerian workers in the past decade did not save 7.5% of their relatively low earnings to fund the so-called infrastructural development of the state as being canvassed by new funds scavengers like Maina. On the contrary, workers voluntarily contribute to pension fund every month against the raining days, for life after work up to retirement age through their respective Retirement Saving Accounts (RSAs).

Workers' RSAs must be protected at all costs failing which Nigeria might witness a national pension strike. Nigerian workers are currently witnessing all forms of wage theft either by short changed payments, delayed payments, diverted pay and bare faced pay official robbery. Any additional pension theft through dubious pensions "for infrastructural developments schemes" or phony top-down social insurance scams as being proposed by Maina will be one pension /wage theft unacceptable and clearly provocative.

Nigerian pensioners especially in the public sector are already caught between the two extremes, namely official government neglect and public sympathy, none of which is beneficial to them. Contributory pension scheme, which is now in trillions of naira, is a legitimate hard-earned savings of workers. It is a deferred payment, which both the workers and employers are compelled to set aside so that workers at old age will not be living on some degrading charity as if they are destitute. The challenge lies in how to make the principle of contributory pension work in Nigeria and not undermine it through illegal raid on the fund and sheer diversion to other purposes rather than pension payment as being canvassed by the likes of Maina. Most state governments that can hardly account for monthly federal allocations cannot be further privileged with pension assets. It will be illegal, extortionist, arbitrary and resisted by all the labour/pension Market actors.

Pension Act of 2004 represents a progressive labour legislation because it attempts to address the naughty issue of compensation after work. The scheme is also strong on corporate governance arrangements that are radically different from the past mismanaged public sector schemes; National Pension Commission supervises the Pension Fund Administrators and Custodians.

President Jonathan must put a time line on the activities of the Task Force on pension in the public sector. It is not the amount of billions the task force claims to have recovered. It is not amount of claims and counter-claims of stolen pension funds both the Task Force and the legislators are trading. The critical issue is how many pensioners in the relevant public sector institutions have been paid their pensions and gratuities? This is the critical question the Pension Act of 2004 sets to address. Already PenCom commendably pays some two billion naira monthly to some 60,000 retirees under the new Contributory pension scheme, a radical departure from the hitherto unfunded non-contributory scheme. The president must strengthen the new contributory pension scheme by protecting it against invaders looking for funds for other purposes rather than payment of retirees. Let no one touch or divert pension asset from its legally sanctioned objectives.

Abdulrasheed Maina - in praise of the Senate[*]

Monsieur Abdulrasheed Maina, (the notorious chairman of the presidential Pension Task Force) has inadvertently put doubt on the time-tested popular received wisdom that says; the whole world cannot after all be wrong. From nowhere in the past six months, Maina has declared a one man-war of attrition against the Senate Committee On Establishment & Public Service, the Senate Committee State & Local Government Administration, the entire Senate of the Federal Republic of Nigeria, the Senate President, the Clerk of the Senate, the police, the National Union of Pensioners, (NUP) and of late the Head of Service of the Federation almost in that order. According to him everybody that matters in the public pension mess controversy is wrong while he is right. It is therefore not surprising that like anybody that dares to move against the world for obviously wrong reasons, Maina has provoked unprecedented star-words of recriminations and indeed damnations. Witness the Senate President, David Mark:

> "...there are a lot of characters in this country who are just pathological liars and professional blackmailers. Maina is just an individual who perhaps says much than he can manage, and he has crucified himself. The executive now has to choose between Maina and the Senate. That is the bottom line...Maina's sins are too many to enumerate. When God decided to give people manner, Maina just decided to be absent."

---

[*] *Daily Trust*, Monday 18th February 2013

It is against this background, one must commend the principled stand of the Senate under the leadership of Senate President David Mark that the embattled Chairman of the moribund Pension Reform Task Team (PRTT) accused of complicity in the illegal diversion of almost a trillion naira pension funds meant for pensioners in the country be made to be accountable.

By rightly insisting that Maina be made accountable for his deeds, Nigeria's legislature has proven to be a "useful organ of pubic opinion as well as 'the nation's committee for handling public grievances. Activist constant legislative check on the Executive impunity has truly made Nigeria's democratic process come of age.

The insistence of 107 senators on police enforcement of the warrant of arrest on the renegade Assistant Director shows that there is no hiding place for scavengers of the nation's pension assets. As yours sincerely has argued before, President Goodluck Jonathan has the responsibility to safeguard the nation's assets as well as pay the huge pension liabilities of millions of pensioners in the public sector. The President must strengthen and support institutions that safeguard the interests of pensioners such as the Senate and its relevant committees and most importantly National Pension Commission, Pencom. The presidency must not provide sanctuary for some individuals accused of criminally diverting pension funds and undermining the pension market.

Stakeholders including the organized labour led by NLC have watched with utter dismay how Abdulrasheed Maina serially defied public summon by the Senate Joint Committee on Establishment and States and Local Governments during its public hearing on public pension administration. Also clearly unacceptable is the way and manner the controversial chairman of what is supposed to be a short term presidential task force had carried on as if the task force (meant to manage police pension fund mess and which clearly lacks any legal backing whatsoever!) has come to stay permanently. Presidential task force cannot and should not be another alternative pension commission in the country. There is only one regulatory pension commission and that is National Pension Commission, PenCom established by an Act of National Assembly in 2004.

Maina made ill informed, unguarded commentaries on the accumulated pensions assets contributed through the hard earned savings of Nigerian workers in both the private and public sectors of the economy in the past eight years the Pension Reform Act of 2004 came into being. For instance he was quoted as saying that about 3 trillion naira pension assets already built in the pension system commendably managed by PENCOM should be made available to the government for so-called infrastructural development in clear violation of pension reform Act of 2004 and investment rules guiding pension fund in the country.

Pension funds assets (contributed by close to 6 million workers) is a contributory funds by workers for pension after work. Nigerian workers in the past decade did not save 7.5% of their relatively low earnings to fund the so-called infrastructural development of the state as being canvassed by new funds scavengers like Maina. On the contrary, workers voluntarily contribute to pension fund every month against the raining days, for life after work up to retirement age through their respective Retirement Saving Accounts (RSAs).

Nigerian workers have witnessed all forms of wage theft either by short changed payments, delayed payments, diverted pay and bare faced pay official robbery. Any additional pension theft through dubious pensions "for infrastructural developments schemes" will be one pension/wage theft unacceptable and clearly provocative. Contributory Pension scheme which is now in trillions is a legitimate hard earned savings of workers. The challenge lies in how to make the principle of contributory pension work in Nigeria and not undermine it through illegal raid on the fund and sheer diversion to other purposes rather than pension payment as being canvassed by the likes of Maina.

President Jonathan must terminate the activities of the so called Task Force on pension in the public sector. It is not the amount of billions the task force claims to have recovered. It is not the amount of claims and counter claims of stolen pension funds both the Task Force and the legislators are trading. The critical issue is how many pensioners in the relevant public sector institutions have been paid their pensions and gratuities? The president must strengthen the new contributory pension scheme by protecting it against invaders looking for funds for other purposes rather than payment of retirees. Let no one touch or divert pension asset from its legally sanctioned objectives.

Saving the Pensioners[*]

Nigeria Labour Congress (NLC) on Wednesday, April 10, 2013 organizes a one-day protest and mass rally being organised to once again call government attention to the deteriorating condition of pensioners on the old non-contributory pension schemes. The first set of rallies planned for Abuja and the state capitals would commence with Abuja and Lagos. The Congress' protest is inspired by what the NLC said to be refusal of government to engage in social dialogue on the ever worsening plight of pensioners and the crisis of public pension administration with all the attendant fraud and grafts. The issues begging for government attention include the non-payment of outstanding arrears to pensioners, the refusal to enrol several thousand on the Federal Pension Payroll and non-payment of death benefits to deserving next-of-kin. Other reasons are the non-implementation of the 53.4% salary review and the ₦18,000 minimum wage in the payment of pension in the society as well as the full implementation of the Report of the Senate Joint Committee on the pension fraud.

Over the years, NLC always observes December 17th of every year to draw attention to the plight of pensioners. Rallies were often organised by the state councils of the Congress with similar goal of reminding those who still care that life after work in Nigeria is still regrettably miserable. Hundreds of pensioners have died due to lack of money to fend for themselves paradoxically while prosecuted and convicted pension directors (read; pension thieves) with billions of Naira pension funds are being granted judicial pardon, as it were

---

[*] *Daily Trust*, 8th April, 2013

166

given fines and sentences that are inversely rated to their respective crimes.

If public retired employees are so much humiliated and invariably being turned into destitutes, then the plights of some retirees in the private sector, (heaven of exploitation) is better imagined.

We must therefore commend NLC under Abdulwaheed Omar for reminding us, (if only one day by way of strike and protest), that we are not only unjust to serving working men and women of Nigeria but we are inexplicably callous in our (mal)treatment of our grandparents and parents called pensioners.

Pensioners' lot represents the worst dimension of crisis of compensation, yours truly reflected upon last week. The truth is that ultimately every working man and woman must get fatigue one day. Whether we want it or not, senility must eventually replace today's abundant energy. Hence the need to prepare for the proverbial raining days by setting aside some funds that will at least meet the subsistence needs of the aged workers. The above constitute the principles that informed the establishment of pension in the public sector. These principles are still certainly valid today. With the collapse of the extended family support and traditional values of historic care and concern for the aged especially since the beginning of notorious structural adjustment, every active and young worker today can only ignore the issue of pension scheme at the instance of his/her sustenance after work. Pension schemes constitute an important and integral part of total compensation for workmen and women.

The truth of the matter is that pensioners are caught between the two extremes, namely official government neglect and public sympathy, none of which is beneficial to them. Pension is a legitimate right of workers. It is a deferred payment, which both the workers and employers must set aside so that workers at old age will not be living on some charity as if they are destitute. The challenge lies in how to make this principle work in Nigeria. The bane of public sector pension lies in its non-contributory character as well as sheer corruption and diversion of funds even allegedly for partisan political purposes. The pension scheme is still regulated by obsolete Pensions Act of 1979 with all its amended provisions. NLC protest is legitimately directed against this much abused public pension scheme NOT the 2004 contributory scheme which has proven to be viable and sustainable.

In fact the protest is also in defence of the accumulated Pension funds assets (contributed by close to 6 million workers) totalling some trillions of naira under the new scheme against pension fund predators. Workers' RSAs under the new scheme must be protected at all costs.

Pension Act of 2004 represents a progressive labour legislation because it attempts to address the naughty issue of compensation after work. The scheme is also strong on corporate governance arrangements that are radically different from the past mismanaged public sector schemes; National Pension Commission supervises the Pension Fund Administrators and Custodians.

President Jonathan must have the political will to clear the arrears under the old pension scheme, apprehend and punish pension offenders. It is not the amount of billions the task force claims to have recovered. It is not amount of claims and counter-claims of stolen pension funds both the Task Force and the legislators are trading. The critical issue is how many pensioners in the relevant public sector institutions have been paid their pensions and gratuities? This is the critical question the Pension Act of 2004 sets to address. Already PenCom commendably pays some two billion naira monthly to some 60,000 retirees under the new Contributory pension scheme, a radical departure from the hitherto unfunded non-contributory scheme. The president must strengthen the new contributory pension scheme by protecting it against invaders looking for funds for other purposes. NLC protest in a sense is therefore also to safeguard the new contributory pension scheme against those who killed the old scheme.

Africa's Premier Trade Union, OATUU at 40[*]

The Organization of African Trade Union Unity (OATUU) marked its 40th anniversary recently. Founded in 1973 (under the defunct Organization of African Unity formed a decade earlier), the formation of OATUU brought to the fore the significance of trade unions in Africa. Unlike contemporary Africa when some governments keep labour at arms length, irrespective of their ideological persuasions, Africa's founding fathers (and mothers too!) appreciated the role of labour in anti-colonial struggles. Even more remarkable too, scores of nationalists and patriots who fought for independence were tested trade unionists in their own rights. Notable historic figures included late Ahmed Sekou Toure of Guinea, a trade unionist turned a political activist. He singularly mobilized the Guinean people for independence and terminated French colonialism in 1958 in a French Referendum. That was a heroic feat given that the likes of the late Félix Houphouet-Boigny in of Ivory Coast voted for continued French rule. The late President Julius Nyerere and former President Kenneth Kaunda, were all unionists who fought against British colonialism in Tanzania and Zambia respectively. Late Tom Mboya led Kenyan Trade Union Movement but was also in the fore front of the struggle for Kenya's Independence. Late President Modibo Keita of Mali, President Kwame Nkrumah of Ghana, Hamani Diori, the founding President of Niger, late Nnamdi Azikiwe, late Chief Obafemi Awolowo, Mallam Aminu Kano and of course, late Pa Michael Imoudu were all union organisers who

---

[*] *Daily Trust*, 22nd April, 2013

brought to bear their respective trade unions skills in contestation and negotiation to lower the British Union Jack. Even in later day liberated territories of Namibia and South Africa, trade unions were the touch bearers in the battle for freedom.

In recognition of the historic positive roles of African Trade Unions in 1973, OAU encouraged and consummated the formation of the OATUU. The Government of Osagyfo Dr. Kwame Nkrumah was even exceptionally appreciative by building a six-storey-building, "Hall of Trade Unions" for the Ghana Trades Union Congress. It is not by accident that OATUU has its secretariat in Accra until recently headed by Alhaji Hassan Sunmonu, the founding President of NLC.

The selling point of OATUU is the unity of Africa's trade union centres. African workers had always desired a continental organization as countervailing force to governments and employers who were equally organised at continental levels taking decisions that impact often negatively on jobs, wages and pensions among others. Trade unions were not immune from the ideological divisions of the Cold war era. Indeed they were atomised into the defunct All-African Trade Union Federation (AATUF), the African Trade Union Confederation (ATUC), and Pan-African Workers' Congress. OATUU is commendably an offshoot of these centres in 1973.

Sadly I search in vain for some discernible perspectives on OATUU at 40. Not long ago, African media uncritically downloaded the mantra according to President Barack Obama that Africa needs strong institutions not strong men. How can we build strong institutions in Africa, when we even lack knowledge of our institutions? OATUU with its secretariat in Accra (interestingly where the American President delivered his sermon about strong institutions in 2009) had been a strong and tested institution with committed selfless working men that included, Denis Akumu of Central Organisation of Trade Unions COTU (K) in Kenya, Hassan Sunmonu of Nigeria Labour Congress (NLC) among others.

OATUU, despite challenges of governance (military dictatorships in many countries until the latest democratization) and unfavourable economic climate (SAP) had made positive impact on the lives of African working men and women. Proudly African, it has helped affiliates (South Sudan reportedly being the newest 55 member) to build capacity, especially in economic literacy. We must credit OATUU and other progressive organizations with the African debt cancellations and debts write offs at the turn of the century. As far back as late eighties, at a time it was fashionable for SAP-imposed military regimes to outdo each other in slavish diligent repayments of dubious debts (even as they denied minimum wages and employment at home!) it is to the credit of the OATUU it called for the unconditional and total cancellation of Africa's debt. It has also been counted on the labour market institution building in the continent. OATUU played a decisive role in the transformation of hitherto top-down OAU Conference of Ministers of Labour and Social Affairs into a more participatory present-day tripartite OAU/AU Labour and Social Affairs Commission. Structural Adjustment programmes (SAPs) of the 1980s collapsed due to the great struggles of OATUU's affiliates notably NLC of Nigeria and TUC of Ghana. In particular NLC since 1988 had been resisting incessant fuel prices increases and leading "SAP riots" even at the risk of the illegal dissolution of its Executive twice under IBB and Abacha dictatorships.

With the support of the Chinese, the OATUU has also built a Labour College in Ghana. Rightly many would question the independence of OATUU if African workers and governments cannot build its infrastructure. If OATUU's Affiliates independently built their offices, why not OATUU? OATUU should avoid the pitfall of the dependency mentality of African leaders who preside over capital flight and corruption in the continent yet still rely on the Chinese government to rebuild AU secretariat in Addis Ababa. Let us copy China and not ape China. Co-operation and partnership, not servitude. In the next 40 years, OATUU must consolidate on unity of actions in defence of rights of African workers. We are again sadly back to proliferation of trade union centres without ideological claims but comfort zones of labour aristocrats. OATUU must also deepen its internal democracy. Its last Congress in Algiers was more of hearsay and murmurs compared to the open democratic contestations and participation that characterized the election of

171

Comrade Alhaji Hassan Sunmonu in late 1980s. OATUU that was loud in the struggle for enthronement of democracy in the continent must reduce its own internal democracy deficits. Brinkmanship alien to trade union movement must give way to comradeship and continental solidarity. Long Live OATUU!

Towards the ILO Centenary[*]

ILO was founded in 1919 after the destructive World War I. It upholds a vision of the world based on social justice. It marks 100th anniversary in the next six years; 2019. This year's 102nd Session of its annual Conference assumes a special and historic significance. Yours comradely delegate served on the Committee of the Conference on Sustainable Development. Importantly too, as the Chairman of the NLC International Relations committee I took the floor at the Plenary which opened on the 12th Wednesday of June in Geneva, Switzerland to discuss the report of ILO Director General. Today I share my intervention with readers on the twin issues of sustainable development and global poverty. Happy reading.

"I bring fraternal greetings from the President of Nigeria Labour Congress (NLC), Comrade Abdulwaheed Omar to the chairperson of ILC and the ILO Director-General, Guy Ryder. I recall with nostalgia that until last year Guy Ryder was a formidable voice in global trade union movement, my constituency! We appreciate the 10th Director General for his report which is truly "concise, clear and accessible". An old received wisdom has it that "He who does not look ahead always remains behind". We commend the Director-General for his comprehensive forward looking realistic report entitled; Towards the ILO centenary; realities, renewal and tripartite commitment. The strength of his vision lies in its profound commendable appreciation of the current realities in the world of work and its proposals for the future. Two issues are of special interests; war against extreme poverty and sustainable development

* *Daily Trust* 17 June, 2013

to the NLC. This report rightly deals with the issue of extreme poverty and prosperity. It is now fashionable to lament the plight of the poor. But it was ILO which first commendably raised the alarm about the danger of global poverty. And that was at a time it was not fashionable and even risky to do so! United States of America did not join the ILO until 1934 under President Franklin Roosevelt. It actually once labelled the moderate lofty human ideals of ILO "communist" and "inimical to free enterprise". ILO Objectives in the Declaration of Philadelphia in 1944 say it all; poverty anywhere constitutes a danger to prosperity everywhere!

We agree with the optimism of this report that overcoming poverty is clearly surmountable. The cited case is China's dramatic development which has taken millions out of poverty. It is clear that progress is being made in the global struggle to eradicate poverty. The Director General's report is even frank enough to point out the danger of the emergence of what I call the new poor, ironically in a number of middle income countries. "These new contours of poverty and prosperity" task us to critically relook at the ILO mandate. The poor need jobs, incomes, food, housing, schools, electricity, roads, pension, credits not recommendations and conclusions. 6 years into ILO centenary, poverty anywhere remains a danger to prosperity everywhere. The zones breeding terrorism are also poverty zones of the world. ILO, more than ever before, needs to be more vocal and loud against the extreme wealth of the few in few nations of the world. There is an inverse relationship between the prosperity of the few and the misery of the many. Many millions of youths and women lack jobs. Many workers do precarious jobs without minimum wages. Many young women and children are pushed into prostitution and child labour. All these unacceptable deprivations take place in a number of member-countries of ILO that parade few billionaires and even owners of private jets! We must reverse this trend. The global widening income inequalities undermine the struggle for social justice. "Mahatma Ghandi of India said it all; the world has enough for everyone's need, but not enough for everyone's greed."

At centenary, ILO must throughout the instrument of social dialogue demand for global wealth redistribution to eradicate poverty. Let us moderate extreme prosperity of the few through tripartite social dialogue for wealth redistribution. It is about common sense. There is a Nigerian proverb which says and rightly too that; "It is an unthinking man who achieves prosperity, and then finds with time, that his body can no longer pass through the door." We have downsized the poor enough. The extreme rich must also shed the weight of their excess wealth through reinvestment of idle luxury wealth in sustainable labour intensive industries, public sector institutions, public schools and creation of decent green jobs. "The alcohol that is insufficient for a whole town ought not to intoxicate one man." In the next century, ILO should be celebrating the wealth of nations and peoples of our planet not lamenting the poverty of many and prosperity of the few. We must replace the well-having of the few with the well- being of the many.

We agree with the conclusion of this report that the key out of poverty is decent job. A Nigerian proverb says it all: "Work is anti-dote/remedy to poverty." However without sustainable development there cannot be decent jobs. In many African countries, we have to reinvent development before we can even make it sustainable. There is a new underdevelopment and de-industrialization in Africa. Many African economies are outside development discourse much less sustainable development! Many are neck-deep in corruption. Growth drivers in the continent are in the extractive sectors. Economies that live on extractions of raw materials without value additions pose serious danger to the climate.

ILO's priorities should include the promotion of economic diversification in constituent member states that are currently dependent on export of raw materials. Countries should be encouraged to create value adding green economic activities and create quality jobs through appropriate macro economic and industrial policies. Real sector is increasingly collapsing killing mass jobs. There is a withering away of the working class. Labour standards without working classes are standards in vain! ILO created in the heat of the crisis of the 20th century is hunted with global economic crisis of the 21st century. We need sustainable enterprises to guarantee sustainable jobs. Indeed as ILO celebrates its centenary we need a binding Convention on Sustainable Development. We once again congratulate the DG for his Vision and urge all tripartite members to make it a reality through critical tripartite engagement and cooperation with the DG centenary reform agenda. Long Live ILO!

Nigeria - Amending the Pension Act[*]

On Wednesday June 26, both the Senate Committee on Establishment and the House of Representatives Committee on Pensions will hold a Joint Public Hearing on the proposed amendments of the Pension Reform Act of 2013 (PRA13). The Bill has since passed the Second (2nd) Reading of both the Senate and the House.

The hope is that the public hearing will promote better conversation about the Pension Act of 2004 and the proposed amendments. The public hearing must lift all stakeholders out of the polarization of the pension discourse of the recent times to some greater common sense about income adequacy for working men and women after retirement. The truth is that ultimately every working woman and working man must get fatigue one day; senility must eventually replace today's abundant energy. Hence the need to prepare for the proverbial raining days by setting aside some funds that will at least meet the subsistence needs of the aged workers. The above constitutes the main principle that informs the establishment of any pension scheme.

The principle of income adequacy for retiree is ever valid whether the scheme takes the form of publicly funded/administered pay-go defined benefit (DB) or privately administered mandatory individual defined contributions (DC). The point cannot be overstated that hundreds and even thousands of pensioners have died due to lack of money to fend for themselves. Paradoxically this tragedy takes place almost simultaneously the prosecuted and

---

[*] *Daily Trust* 24 June, 2013

convicted pension directors (read; pension thieves) with billions of stolen pension funds are being granted judicial cover with fines and sentences that are inversely rated to their respective crimes. If public retired employees are so much humiliated and invariably being turned into destitute, then the plights of some retirees in the private sector, (heaven of exploitation) is better imagined. The public hearing must be conducted against the background of the need for reform, reform and reform of pension. Indeed we need pension revolution, not just reform. Happily the notable drivers of this week public hearing are already converted to reform agenda. In fact, the Chairman of the Senate Joint Committee on Public Service and Establishment and State and Local Government Administration, Senator Aloysius Etok (PDP, Akwa Ibom North-West) that investigated the pension scam last year truly distinguished himself for his singular sense of purpose, courage and commitment in the face of intimidation and threats of the pension thieves. It was to his credit and his committee that it was revealed that a total of ₦273.9billion pension funds had been misappropriated between 2005 and 2011. All these revelations about the public sector pension scam show that we must urgently think outside the box of unfunded, crime-prone defined benefit (DB). The future lies in the mandatory individual defined contributions (DC) which the Pension reform Act represents.

Pension is a legitimate right of workers. It is a deferred payment, which both the workers and employers must set aside so that workers at old age will not be living on some charity as if they are destitute. The challenge lies in how to make this principle work in Nigeria. The bane of public sector pension lies in its non-contributory character as well as sheer corruption and diversion of funds even allegedly for partisan political purposes. The pension scheme is still regulated by obsolete Pensions Act of 1979 with all its amended provisions. NLC protest over pension is legitimately directed against this much abused public pension scheme *not* the 2004 contributory scheme which less than ten years has proven to be viable and sustainable. With almost 3.8 trillion naira contributed by as many as five million workers, the Pension Reform Act represents a progressive labour legislation because it attempts to address the naughty issue of reserve compensation fund after work. Pension Act rightly legitimizes a sustainable contributory scheme compared to the moribund non-contributory scheme. The challenge lies in further widening the scope of coverage to include more states, private sector establishments as well as the informal sector. Thus the new review should curtail exemptions and withdrawals.

On the contrary, the new amendments must promote more inclusions. The Pension Act is also strong on corporate governance arrangements; National Pension Commission supervises the Pension Fund Administrators totalling 20 today. There is the urgent need to review the *penalties* and s*anctions* for non-compliance by some employers, who either deduct but do not remit to the PFAs. Stiffer penalties are certainly desirable against mismanagement or diversion of pension funds assets. The rates of contributions are also due for a review equitably with employers paying more than the workers. All these and other critical issues that will deepen the pension reform must dominate the public hearings. The five million workers already captured under the reform are commendable. But this number is a far cry from 80 million-strong potential workforce in Nigeria. The three trillion naira funds contributed so far can hardly meet the future income adequacy of retirees, which underscores the need for more reform and not less.

Rethinking the Senate Constitution Amendment on Labour*

The famous quote of the 16th U.S. President (1861-65), Abraham Lincoln according to which "Democracy is the government of the people, by the people, for the people" was turned upside last week to mean amending the Constitution by the few (109) senators to advance the obscene privileges of a legislative cabal.

Nigeria's 7th Senate in pursuit of crass class interest exclusively approved Life pension for the principal Assembly officials namely; Senate President and Deputy Senate President as well as former Speakers and Deputy Speakers of the House of Representatives while in the same breadth removed the *labour* and *pension* rights of 85 million Nigerian working men and women from the exclusive list of 1999 Constitution with a view of making working life precarious, deregulated and unprotected, certainly not better. Abraham Lincoln who was also credited with the emancipation of the slaves between 1809 and 1865 would have chuckled in his grave to realise that some self serving slave drivers have re-grouped at the Senate of the Federal Republic of Nigeria some 200 years after the emancipation of slaves.

The challenge is whether Nigerian workers would allow the few who claim to have been elected from their respective constituencies to make law for good governance go with such arrogant and insensitive legislative impunity which through constitutional amendment throw the majority to the dogs while shielding their own privileges with constitutional clauses. Removing the basic rights of majority of working people from hitherto mainstream exclusive list and pushing them on the margins of the concurrent states list

---

* *Daily Trust*, July 22, 2013

definitely does violence to the concept of democracy as a majority rule.

The ill-informed decision to remove the power of the Federal government to exclusively make law on labour matters also shows the poverty of knowledge among our legislators about labour market issues and their relevance to national development. Minimum wage is only one important labour matters. Others include trade unions, industrial relations, conditions, safety and welfare of working men and women. Nigeria wants to be part of the twenty leading developed economies of the world. No serious country that is genuinely committed to development agenda would casually step down issues bordering on labour motivation and productivity from national mainstream agenda to some footloose concurrent List as chaotic as Nigeria's states.

World wide the laws which govern labour matters have significant impact on growth and development. Even Lord Lugard recognised the importance of labour as a factor of production and development. The first Federal (note; not state!) Ministry to be established was Federal Ministry of Labour. And that was in 1914. The colonial authority as well as post independent Nigerian governments recognised that labour motivation and productivity was a critical success factor for transformation. Thus all labour laws with respect to trade unions and industrial conflicts were regulated and managed centrally for development. Behind the celebrated miracle of Nigeria's double digit growth plus development in the 1960s and 1980s were progressive labour laws regulating minimum wages and pensions as well as collective bargaining and industrial conflicts.

With the current high level of unemployment, worsening poverty, unregulated immigration, foreign investment of dubious value and underdevelopment, rampant strikes and industrial conflicts, more than ever before Nigeria needs a federally-managed (not deregulated) labour process sanctioned by the Constitution. 1999 Constitution commendably retains the progressive legacy of Nigeria's constitutional process which from Independence had always known that labour plays a vital role in the mobilisation of the working people for growth development and thus puts labour on the exclusive list of the constitution. This means only the federal government can and must legislate on labour matters. This explains why Nigeria's Labour laws are among the most progressive in the world even with all the challenges of implementations and interpretations. Since the country became independent and a member of the United Nations and subsequently the International Labour Organisation (ILO), being a unique arm of the UN system, Nigeria labour law have largely reflected standards set by ILO conventions and recommendations in respect of labour matters. It is significant that even during the military regimes, when draconian labour decrees are made, they were made by the Federal government not deregulated and left to the whims of ever divergent states of the federation. The combined effects of these legislations over the years have helped to strengthen the country's industrial relations system, trade union institutions and have made the unions formidable social partners in national development process. The latest proposed amendment to step down labour matters to the state and village levels shows that the Senate does not appreciate labour as an "essential and integral part of our national development structure," an asset to be national cultivated for development.

In pursuance of the economic and democratic aspiration of the country, Nigeria must have labour policies that encourage and strengthen national, international, independent, democratic, transparent and accountable trade unions, not fragmented and deregulated labour process with all the attendant implications for industrial crises. Trade union laws should also be fair, balanced and consistent with ratified ILO conventions. In addition, effective labour administration and freely collective bargaining should be the main determinants of terms and conditions of employment to ensure sustainable industrial peace and equitable reward system. Nigeria must achieve excellent labour management and industrial relations that would promote industrial harmony, tripartism and commitment to work and productivity. All the above can only be possible if labour is treated as an exclusive and important factor of development. The House of Representatives has shown over the years to be closer to the people.

It must retain labour on the exclusive Federal List just like other progressive constitutions of the world. The House must last reject the temptation of a greed clause that gives life privileges to few Assembly chieftains at the expense of a worsening economy and mass deprivation.

ASUU Strike: crisis of Collective Bargaining*

The strike by the Academic Staff Union of Universities (ASUU) enters the third month.

Somehow the strike has become the issue rather than the real issues that made the union apply the same strike weapon it has over the last three decades adopted to demand for the reinvention of the university education. Re-invention precisely because there was once a country (apology to Chinua Achebe) that was truly a knowledge destination. The pioneer universities and polytechnics (which we could then count on our finger tips!) truly were centres of uninterrupted knowledge service delivery. Indeed it was unthinkable for intellectual workers like the respected ASUU members to be active in trade unionism no less for them to deploy the last weapon of mass industrial disruption; strikes. Students of trade union struggles for better working conditions will call that ASUU as it is today was not known in the 1960s, 1970s, when blue collar workers in the civil service (Nigeria Civil Service Union formed in 1912 being the first legal union in Nigeria) and railway men (no women then!) in Nigeria Union of Railwaymen were up in protests and strikes for better working conditions.

Indeed in the 1960s and 1970s when textile workers were engaging in go- slows, and strikes to demand for right to unionise, universities were seen as exclusive Ivory Towers, (not necessary inclusive poor working environments of today) such that most academics had no need for a union not to talk of the one that would go on strikes like blue collar workers. As a matter of historic fact,

---

* *Daily Trust*, 16 September 2013

academics formed Association for some social get together during this period out of choice unlike today that they are members of the ASUU out of necessity to press home the demands for basic things like good remuneration, pension and above all funding of the universities. Certainly universities' lecturers never joined the great strikes of 1964 for costs of living allowances as well as the Udoji 'awards' of 1973. That was developmentalist Nigeria, which funded education, nurtured universities' staff as a critical success factor for cultivating the necessary human resources through adequate pay and incentives for learning and research. Of course there were few occasional closures of universities as it was in 1977, during the Alli-Must-Go when the first assault was launched against education through budget cut and subsidy removal. Even then universities' calendar that year ran as students still graduated and called for the mandatory one year national service. What then must have gone wrong? Why would a poorer Nigeria of the 1960s and 1970s guarantee uninterrupted educational service delivery why a richer Republic of 2013 shut down the universities for three months and even as long as nine months during Abacha era? My interest in this series is purely academic. Interestingly the ASUU's struggle is the struggle of academics. At the core of the ongoing crisis in the universities is the issue of collective bargaining. But before then, we must ask the question; do human resources really matter in Nigeria? If oil and gas sector had been shut down for three months can the federal and state governments remain indifferent the way they are to the current ASUU strike?

Nigeria is legitimately ambitious to be one of the leading 20 economies in 2020, just seven years' time. However, we often define development narrowly in terms of huge infrastructure and macro economic factors such as growth rate (7.5%, one of the highest in the world!) GDP, Nigeria being Africa's second biggest GDP of $232 billion. As significant as these economic numbers are, one critical success factor missing in our discussion is the quantity and quality of 165 million human resources which will drive development agenda. Despite the inventions of computers, iPad, Internet, labour remains a critical factor of sustainable development. Indeed China (certainly one of the 10 developed economies) boasts of 1.5 billion human resources not necessarily oil and gas. Any organization or country that ignores constant motivation of human resources through constant capacity building risks unnecessary work-place conflicts and low productivity. If we want to be part of the leading economies in 2020, we must ask if the universities of the remaining 19 countries are closed like Nigeria. If the universities of other countries are functioning, certainly Nigeria is out of the race to the top of the 20 in 2020. Paradoxically, collective bargaining which is the tool for industrial conflict resolution is part of the industrial relations heritage of Nigeria. Nigeria has ratified Core ILO conventions 98, 151 and 154 dealing with terms of work covered by collective bargaining. Convention 98 is fundamental because it underscores the application of the principles of the right to organize and to bargain collectively and freely.

Nigeria has a vibrant collective bargaining process which has guaranteed relative industrial harmony in the work place. With vibrant bargaining agents, namely trade unions, and employers' Associations, and hundreds of thousands collective agreements signed annually, Nigeria is an industrial harmony destination. Industrial harmony does not preclude strikes and conflicts. Harmony means when disputes occur, through collective bargaining; contestation can lead to resolution and accommodation later. The first step in negotiating a new collective agreement or in reviewing an existing collective agreement involves preparation of proposals. A proposal is a comprehensive statement of demands put forward by the union or employers association for the consideration of the employer or unions. In preparing the proposal, the needs of the workers and industry are considered, so also is the position of the economy and the profitability and performance of the industries. A well researched proposal is likely to hasten the process of negotiation rather than a proposal that is based on guess work. It is important to note that a proposal is *not* an agreement; it is only a list of demands submitted for negotiation. How does the universities' crisis fit into this theoretical model?

What about Industrial Relations?*

Last weekend yours truly returned to National Institute of Policy and Strategic Studies, (NIPPS) Kuru Jos as a discussant of the paper ably delivered by His Excellency, Comrade Governor of Edo State, Adams Oshiomhole, *mni* on the "Challenges of Industrial Relations, Labour Productivity and National Development in Nigeria." It was homecoming for both the Comrade Governor who attended Senior Executive Course (SEC) 9 in 1989 and yours truly who with the encouragement of Comrade Governor (then President of NLC) attended Senior Executive Course (SEC) 27 in 2005. It was nostalgia to have an interactive session with the current participants of SEC. NO. 36. Profound appreciation goes to the Institute ably led by the DG Professor Tijani Mohammed Bande, OFR for choosing the theme for this year's course: "Challenges of Industrial Relations, Labour Productivity and National Development in Nigeria." Somehow, *industrial relations* are becoming an endangered concept. It is commendable that NIPSS brings back the concept of *industrial relations*. Nigeria's contemporary world of work has become industry-shy and indeed *Industrial Relations* blind. No thanks to the culture of sharing and corruption as distinct from culture of production and value addition of the post-Independence era. Even up to the early 1990s, industrial relations studies in our universities were as important in ranking as studies in law and businesses. The deafening collapse of industries caused by uncontrolled globalization and new forms of employment relations such as out-sourcing, casualisation and neo-liberal thinking that questions the essence of work

---

* Monday 31 March 2014

altogether, industrial relations studies assume less importance. Neo-liberalism which preaches liberalization, monetization, downsizing, privatization, lean government and the notorious philosophy that government has no business with business has done much violence to the concept of industrial relations. Of course there can be no relations between employers and employees, or between employees and employees in the industry when industry collapses or non-existent. Nor can there be industrial relations when we only talk of "labour market" where the relations are often impersonal and less guided by any rules and regulations. It is certainly commendable that your NIPSS has set us thinking about the need to reinvent the industry and possibly reinvent industrial relations which we all know deals with all the complexity of relations at work particularly the relationship between the management and workers, workers and workers and even mangers and managers. There is an urgent need for Nigeria and indeed Africa to reinvent industry and industrialization if we must reinvent industrial relations.

Paradoxically, notwithstanding our preference to ignore production issues and be industrial relations-shy, we are ever hunted by the spectre of industrial relations crisis. Much has been said about the suspension of Sanusi Lamido former Governor of the Central Bank of Nigeria. Most commentaries deal on the suspension deal with the reasons for the suspension, the most controversial being the alleged missing funds. Few touched at the heart of the matter; employment/industrial relations. President Umaru Musa Yar'Adua nominated Sanusi on 1st June 2009. His appointment was confirmed by the Senate on 3 June 2009 in a record time. President Goodluck Ebele Jonathan on Thursday, 20th February 2014 suspended him from office few months to the end of an eventful, albeit controversial single 5-year term he had preferred. As a labour market student, it's of profound academic interest of how a process driven easy entry (with appointment and senate confirmation) of a chief central banker was inversely related to his suspension/exit without recourse to the same process that brought him to office. Secondly why will the suspension of the Governor of the CBN, impact so much on the financial market as much as the collapse of capital shares? Certainly employment relations have a lot of implications for development.

In the final analysis workers who are deserving of decent works, well paid for, secured with easy entry and exit.

International Labour Organization (ILO) has shown over the years that millions of workers worldwide live on precarious works that are poorly remunerated. They get fired and hired at the behest of employers. The recent casualization of the CBN's governor has certainly made another case for decent protected work for the driver, a messenger no less for a CBN governor. The point cannot be overstated that there is a direct relationship between industrialization, employment and poverty eradication. In fact there is no way Nigeria can meaningfully address the problem of poverty without addressing the production issues driven by human resources. As important as oil and gas industry and solid mineral resources may be, they are exhaustible. In any case there are abundant evidences to show that extractive industries are the curse rather than blessings for sustainable development in developing countries. Employment is a derived factor. The challenge therefore is to revive the real productive sectors of the economy and creatively engage the unemployed in value-adding activities. It has long been recognized that there are positive linkages between harmonious labour-management relations and productivity increase. The hallmark of any productive and profitable organization rests on effective and peaceful Labour/Management relations. This is so because where there is no understanding between Labour and Management, the environment for working conscientiously to improve productivity cannot exist. Where employers and workers cooperate on the basis of mutual trust and confidence, it is easier for them to agree on corporate policies and practices designed for productivity and competitiveness improvement and to implement participatory approaches to productivity improvement at the workplace. Witness the recent endless strikes in all sectors of the economy! On the other hand, where labour-management relations are influenced by mistrust, adverse attitudes and confrontation, productivity drives have little chance to succeed. The situation is particularly serious where opposition and confrontation lead to open conflicts and disputes which are likely to further deteriorate labour management relations, disrupt production processes/service delivery, and in some cases lead to collective work stoppages.

What about Industrial Relations? (2)[*]

With posthumous apology to Chinua Achebe, there was certainly once a Nigeria with abundant data on valued added activities (productivity) and work related relations in general. For instance industrial disputes statistics and the associated man hours, sorry (to be gender correct-) human hours!) losses were once part of national statistics. There was once a productive Nigeria in which industrial progress was valued and the inherent industrial relations between employers and employees and even employees and employees are captured in quantitative and qualitative data. Value addition through productivity or any value subtraction through strikes and industrial disruptions were measured in terms of times and money. For as long as it lasted, the moribund Federal Office of Statistics (FOS) was very active in compiling useful labour market data in the 1960s up to the 1980s, and even up the 1990s.

These data in turn served as useful guide in managing industrial relations. Same for the Annual Reports of Central Bank of Nigeria (CBN). Undoubtedly Nigeria Bureau of Statistics (NBS) under the able leadership of the Statistician General, Dr. Yemi Kale, has truly modernized. We now have an on-line e-Library of statistics to match! I am therefore surprised to have searched in vain for some basic data on industrial disputes for instance in its posted Annual Abstract of Statistics of 2011. For a country that daily muddles through from one avoidable industrial dispute to the other, it is not clear why NBS is labour disputes data blind. If we cannot count it (read; labour dispute!) we certainly can hardly tame it! Even the quick links on

---

[*] Monday April 17, 2014

socio-economic data indicate nothing on industrial disputes. The Bureau that remarkably assembles good data on capital flow, inflation, exchange rates and even on once-in-many-life times development agenda paradigm such as Millennium Development Goals (MDGs) inexplicably has little on offer on industrial relation. NBS seems to assume that only the Federal Ministry of Labour and Productivity should gather the labour data. This smacks of class bias. Data on labour are needed just as data on other factors of productions are readily available. One of the challenges of industrial relations therefore is paucity of data on critical industrial relations especially on industrial disputes. Participants of Senior Executive Course (SEC) 36 must impress on NBS to add robust industrial relations data to its Abstract. Statistics are urgently needed on national Productivity, Collective Bargaining and collective agreements, job classifications, wages and settlements, Industrial conflicts and conflict resolutions, Pension and Social Security, Occupational health and safety, grievances at work and all that make up industrial relations. These data must also be disaggregated between private and public sectors for informed judgments on policy.

The point cannot be overstated! Nigeria is hunted by a spectre of (in most cases) avoidable industrial relations crises. Primary school teachers and Academic lecturers are periodically on strikes. These strikes average 3 months annually in the last two decades. In certain years universities are shut for six months! Currently seven months old strikes of the polytechnics seem forgotten. So much then for primary and tertiary educational service delivery! The health sectors at Federal and state levels have been in industrial turmoil of varying dimension as doctors, nurses, pharmacists had to go on strikes at different times. Hitherto the blue collar workers in the private sectors were known for work stoppages given the precarious nature of private sector caused by employment based on morbid exploitation for maximum profits by the owners of enterprises. However in recent times, the private sector seems relatively more stable given the entrenched process of collective bargaining and conflict resolution put in place over the years. Work is also getting precarious in the public sector making it strike prone. Even the so-called essential services such as the police attempted strikes in 2002 during OBJ first term. Interestingly too, the labour unions are also getting strike fatigue. Just last week, Nigeria Labour Congress (NLC) under the leadership of its President, Abdulwaheed Omar, in Abuja counselled the Independent Petroleum Marketers Association of Nigeria (IPMAN) against an abuse of strike weapon by the petroleum marketers who are at war over leadership of (IPMAN). Nigeria parades remarkable labour market institutions and significant labour laws that should regulate industrial relations. These institutions include tripartite National Labour Advisory Council (NLAC) made up of trade unions NLC and TUC, employers' Association, NECA, states and federal governments), Industrial Arbitration Panel (IAP), National Industrial Court, NIC. There are scores of collective bargaining councils in the private sector. These institutions are to mediate and reconcile labour market actors in disputes. Nigeria has also ratified and indeed domesticated core labour conventions 87 and 98, 151 and 154 dealing with terms of work covered. Participants of Senior Executive Course (SEC) 36 have the singular research task of explaining the gap between robust institutions and rules and industrial relations performance. Speaking on the 2013 ministerial mid-term report platform, the Minister of Labour and Productivity, Emeka Wogu reported a total of 398 labour related grievances and trade disputes between 2011 and 2013. Unofficial statistics would reveal that labour related disputes are in thousands within these periods. And at what cost? We are inundated with corruption as distinct from development narratives. Therefore it is easier to quantify billions of naira lost to fuel subsidy robbery, pension and crude oil thefts. But we should also acknowledge the lost of billions of what the great political economist, Paul Baran, in his classic, *Political Economy of Growth*, called potential surplus due (in this case) to human hours lost to strikes and work stoppages. Next week we conclude by looking at the causes of these strikes. The issue is not a blame game among labour market actors but to point out that whoever causes them the result is the same; productivity haemorrhage for an economy striving to overcome massive poverty and willing to be part of leading 20 developed economies in 2020!

Building Up Workers' Power: 3ʳᵈ ITUC World Congress*

The Third ITUC World Congress opened yesterday, 18 May, at the City Cube in Berlin, Germany. As a delegate of Nigeria Labour Congress, yours comradely witnessed the historic opening ceremony of what the ITUC President, Michael Sommer aptly dubbed "United Nations of Working people". Over 1500 trade unionists representing 176 million workers from 161 countries are attending the 3rd International Trade Union Confederation World Congress which takes place from May 18 to 23rd.

The Congress which represents millions of organized workforce from Europe, Asia, Africa, Latin America as well as America meets every four years. ITUC is the largest democratic organisation in the world representing 325 national trade unions and working people all over the world. The 2014 theme is "Building Workers' Power". The opening ceremony received addresses from German Foreign Minister Frank-Walter Steinmeier and Helen Clark, UNDP Administrator, representing the United Nations, and ITUC President Michael Sommer. All the addresses stressed the need for fairer redistribution of the global wealth, global peace and and to terrorism. Earlier the ITUC General Secretary's address by Sharan Burrow outlined the state of the world for working people and the findings of the ITUC Global Poll 2014. The Congress also witnessed the presence of ILO Director-General Guy Ryder who will address the Congress today.

Delegates are expected to debate organising campaigns in multi-national companies including T-Mobile USA and Deutsche Telekom, organising in the informal sector, government action plans to address

---

* Monday May 19ᵗʰ, 2014

194

inequality including a minimum living wage and social protection, climate action and trade agreements. The Congress will also hold a public vote for the worst employer-boss in the world. There will also be workers' hearings on the informal sector and discrimination and panel debates on indigenous rights, domestic workers. A new global rights index will be released on the worst countries for workers based on violations recorded from 2013 to 2014.

Special guests include former professional footballers Abdeslam Ouaddou and Zahir Belounis who was trapped in Qatar for 17 months; Gordon Brown MP, UN Special Envoy for Global Education; Jay Naidoo, Chairman of the Global Alliance for Improved Nutrition and a former Minister in the Mandela Cabinet; Professor Ozlem Onaran, Professor of Workforce and Economic Development Policy at University of Greenwich; Larry Elliott, Guardian Economics Editor; and Jayati Ghosh, Professor of Economics at Jawaharlal Nehru University, New Delhi, India. ITUC reported that workers across the globe are losing faith in their national governments whom they see as putting the interests of big corporations ahead of their own, according to a new international public opinion poll from the International Trade Union Confederation (ITUC). Released at the opening of the 3rd ITUC World Congress in Berlin, Sunday 18th May, the ITUC Global Poll 2014 commissioned from market research company TNS Opinion, covers the general public of fourteen countries which have half the world's population. T. Sharan Burrow, General Secretary, International Trade Union Confederation in the report indicates that:

"The global economy needs co-ordinated action to raise living standards around the world. Seven years into the economic crisis has left structural damage to the global economy and the global workforce with more than 200 million people unemployed and many more struggling with low wages. Governments are in the grip of corporate power and are failing their people."

- The poll showed: 79 per cent do not believe the minimum wage is enough for a decent life.

- Some 82 per cent say their wages have fallen behind the cost of living or remained stagnant.
- 88 per cent support lifting the minimum wage in every country around the world.
- "The global labour movement meeting in Berlin at the ITUC World Congress has put entrenched business interests on notice. Nearly two-thirds of people want governments to tame corporate power.
- People, dissatisfied with their own government's performance, know they are increasingly in the grip of corporate power. The world has to change, power needs to be rebalanced.
- Big business and big finance must be tamed or democratically elected governments risk becoming mere puppets in economic and social decisions," said Sharan Burrow. The poll showed growing levels of uncertainty about family income: One in two can't keep up with the rising cost of living.
- Seven out of ten European respondents say their income has not kept up with the cost of living.

In the past three years over half the world's population have not been able to save any money. "Realising decent wages for working families and those on low incomes means tackling the excesses of the 1 %. When people can't save, family security is threatened with no capacity to invest in housing or other assets. Savings represent an essential component of long-term balanced growth," said Sharan Burrow. The poll showed rising levels of concern about job security: One in two have direct or family experience of unemployment. 41 per cent expect their job to be less secure in the next two years.

Only one in two people believe the next generation will find decent jobs. The poll showed distrust in government and the economic system: 68 per cent think their government is doing a bad job at tackling unemployment. Four out of five people (78 per cent) believe the economic system favours the wealthy, rather than being fair to most. More than half rate the current economic situation in their country as bad. "When people increasingly fear for the next generation, it should be a warning for governments to act. People want their governments to reduce the gap between rich and poor, ensure fair wages, and increase job security, the report concludes.

Africa Special Pension Summit[*]

Today in Abuja His Excellency President Goodluck Ebele Jonathan, GCFR will declare open the inaugural edition of the World Pension Summit in Africa. The host is the National Pension Commission (PenCom) which partners with the World Pension Summit to deliver the first ever 'Africa Special' Summit. The Summit, the first of its type also marks the 10th Anniversary of the pension reform in Nigeria that led to the enactment of the Pension Reform Act 2004, introduced the Contributory Pension Scheme (CPS) and established PenCom as the regulator of all pension matters in Nigeria.

Pension is a legitimate right of workers. It is a deferred payment, which both the workers and employers must set aside so that workers at old age will not be living on some charity as if they are destitute. The truth is that ultimately every working woman and working man must get fatigue one day; senility must eventually replace today's abundant energy. Hence the need to prepare for the proverbial raining days by setting aside some funds that will at least meet the subsistence needs of the aged workers. The above constitutes the main principle that informs the establishment of any pension scheme. The challenge lies in how to make this principle work in Nigeria and Africa as a whole.

Pension Act of 2004 passed ten years ago represents a progressive labour legislation because it attempts to address the naughty issue of compensation after work. The principle of income adequacy for retiree is ever valid whether the scheme takes the form of publicly funded/administered pay-go defined benefit (DB) or privately administered mandatory individual defined contributions

* Monday 7th July 2014

(DC). The bane of public sector pension lies in its non-contributory character as well as sheer corruption and diversion of funds even allegedly for partisan political purposes. The contributory pension scheme is strong on corporate governance arrangements that are radically different from the past mismanaged public sector schemes. National Pension Commission supervises the Pension Fund Administrators and Custodians. The successes recorded in the implementation of the CPS have resulted in a fully funded pension scheme that delivers on the promise of timely payment of retirement benefits to retirees, as opposed to the inefficiencies of the past. Pension Assets have reportedly grown to N4.21 trillion as at March 2014. The proportion of the assets to Nigeria's GDP grew from 1.4% in 2006 to 9.5% in 2013, an average yearly growth of 30%. The CPS has generated appreciable pool of long term investable funds for the first time in Nigeria which could be utilized towards reducing the huge infrastructure deficits in the country through safe and secure investible instruments, in tune with the Transformation Agenda of the federal government.

From initially licensed 26 Pension Fund Administrators (PFAs), 7 closed Pension Fund Administrators (CPFAs) and 5 Pension Fund Custodians (PFCs), it is presently reduced to 20 PFAs due to mergers and acquisitions, 7 CPFAs, 4 PFCs, 19 Approved Existing Schemes (AESs). The number of registered contributors was 6.02 million as at the end of March, 2014 with the public sector (including States & LGAs) accounting for 49.71% of the total registrations while Private Sector accounts for 50.29%. In terms of Redemption of Retirement Bonds the sum of N404.32 billion was released by FGN into the RBBRF account with CBN from inception to December, 2013. N410.94 billion redeemed into Retirement Saving Accounts (RSA) of FGN mandatory/voluntary retirees and Next of Kin (NOK) of deceased employees. On payment of retirement benefits, a total number of 86, 628 retirees on Programmed Withdrawal (PW) have been paid as at March, 2014 with FGN Retirees - 66,874, State – 3,746, and Private Sector – 16,008. Similarly, number of retirees on Annuity paid as at March, 2014 amounts to 9,212 (FGN Retirees – 7,270; State Government Retirees – 940; Private Sector Retirees –

1,002). Lump sum payments (PW and Annuity) amount to N236.19 billion as at March, 2014. Average monthly payment for PW is N2.45 billion while Annuity is ₦367.52 million.

The National Pension Commission must be commended for ensuring effective supervision, excellent service delivery through establishment of Zonal Offices, establishment of call centre and collaborating with other regulatory agencies to expand investment outlets and stepped up enforcement activities.

Recently President Goodluck Jonathan commendably signed the Pension Reform Bill 2014 into law at the Presidential Villa, Abuja. The new law, which is meant to govern and regulate the administration of the uniform pension scheme for both public and private sectors in Nigeria, repeals the Pension Reform Act, No.2, 2004 and features new clauses that include the power vested in the pension commission to institute criminal proceedings against employers for persistent refusal to remit pension contributions.

The 2014 Act also empowers PenCom, subject to the fiat of the AGF, to institute criminal proceedings against employers who persistently fail to deduct and/or remit pension contributions of their employees within the stipulated time. This was not provided for by the 2004 Act.

The new law also reviewed upward the penalties and sanctions, having discovered that those provided under the old law were no longer sufficient deterrents against infractions of the law. Significantly the new law allows PenCom to revoke the licence of erring pension operators

Rethinking the Doctors' Mass Sack[*]

Observers of the events in the ever crisis-ridden country's health sector desperately wait to hear something new.

Certainly Nigeria and Nigerians want to read that governments at all levels of responses have successfully sacked the dreaded Ebola disease, contain the new monster or getting closer to a curative vaccine. Certainly the news nobody wants to hear is the mass sack of 16,000 resident doctors in Nigeria and worse still abolition of residency or trainee doctors altogether.

Precisely because the decision of the Federal Government was borne out of frustration rather than an informed sober policy; the government must urgently rethink the action. According to the Permanent Secretary in the Ministry of Health, L.N. Awute, the sack directive was based on an order by President Goodluck Jonathan adding the "letters of termination of residency training" would be served on the resident doctors. He said that the sack came after successive attempts by the Federal Government to reach a consensus with striking doctors under the Nigeria Medical Association (NMA) failed.

He noted that despite successive intervention meetings, the NMA had gone ahead with its protracted strike action with attendant pains to Nigerians in dire need of medical attention. The point cannot be overstated that the NMA has over used the strike weapon over dispute of interests as distinct from dispute of rights. Assuming practicing medicine is a popularity test, very few Nigerians would vote for a Nigerian doctor given the ease with which they abandon

---

[*] Monday 18th August 2014

201

work on account of issues not dealing with pay or core work right agenda but with sector governance issues. One of the demands of the NMA was that the Federal Government through the Ministry of Health should formalize and implement the report of the inter-agency committee on residency training. Another was that the FG must release a uniform template on the appointment of resident doctors and a funding framework for residency training established while overseas clinical attachment be fully restored and properly funded.

Of course these are legitimate demands but the method of pursuing this struggle through indefinite strikes is unacceptable. How earth can you abandon a cancer or accident victim in the name of strike just to get an inter-agency report implemented? As a trade unionist myself, the point must be made that labour market issues should be knowledge driven. Increasingly labour market is becoming an all-comers' territory and the latest comers are the doctors who engage on endless works tapped in a country in which many are looking for work. Dispute of rights dealing with pay and employment requires different approaches to resolve as distinct from dispute of interests that requires sustained campaigns and lobby in a democracy. Doctors are not denied pay, so they cannot deny their patients the services they are being paid under any pretext.

Dictatorship of strikes by doctors is as bad and unacceptable as dictatorship of sack letters by the government. All said government mass sack approach is an unacceptable over kill that will further worsen the crisis in the sector. Coming on the heel of Ebola outbreak begging for more hands, it is self-defeatist. It's time government engaged the doctors further proving them the necessary insurance covers to all with the latest menace of Ebola. Let's sack Ebola not the doctors. Above all both the doctors and the government must be tempered by the miserable Nigeria's health numbers. They include the following:

Life expectancy at birth was estimated at 43.3 years for Nigeria compared to 56.7 years for Ghana and 49 years for South Africa. Infant mortality rate was estimated at 98 per 1000 live births for Nigeria. In Ghana and South Africa, the comparative figures were 59 and 53. Under-five mortality rate per 1000 live births stood at 265 in

Nigeria compared to 186 for Ghana in 2003. The probability at birth of surviving to age 55 for females in Ghana (52.9 per cent) was almost twice that of Nigeria (33.2 per cent). The maternal mortality ratio (adjusted) per 100,000 live births in Nigeria was 800. The corresponding figures for Ghana and South Africa were 540 and 240. By 2003, the maternal mortality ratio in Nigeria had risen to 948/100,000. Indeed, with a range of 339/100,000 to 1.716/100,000) Nigeria's maternal mortality rate is considered to be 'one of the highest in the world' (FMoH Health Sector Reform Programme).

Please by all means let us sack these miserable statistics and not the doctors. But the doctors must also re look at their strategy for welfare improvement beyond the most predictable and increasingly unhelpful endless work stoppages.

The 2014 National Productivity Day[*]

Yours truly was a privileged Guest/Award recipient at this year's 13th National Productivity Day (NPD)/Conferment of National productivity Order of Merit (NPOM) Award.

This is to formally express my sincere appreciation for my nomination by the labour movement and selection by the National Productivity Centre under the leadership of Dr Paul Bdliya, Director for conferment of the NPOM award by His Excellency, Dr Goodluck Ebele Jonathan, GCFR, President and Commander in Chief of the Armed Forces, Federal Republic of Nigeria, which took place on Thursday August 21, 2014 in Abuja.

Yours comradely is appreciative of this singular official recognition of my contribution to nation building. Special thanks to Chief Emeka Wogu, Honourable Minister, whose ministry, Federal Ministry of Labour and Productivity processed the nomination and the Vice President, Muhammad Namadi Sambo who represented the president to confer 2014 NPOM awards on 15 other individuals that included Alhaji Bukar Goni, former Head of Service and Minister of Aviation, Osita Chidoka as well as three organizations, namely Kano State Ministry of Agriculture and Natural Resources, Katsina State Primary Health Care Development Agency and (National Emergency Management Agency) NEMA.

I agree with President Goodluck Jonathan's message on the day that stressed the need for all Nigerians to embrace high productivity in their respective professions to increase the country's economic growth and development. Simply put: Nigeria can improve on its productivity. We must consume what produce, and produce what we

---

[*] Monday 25th August 2014

204

consume and minimize import of what ordinarily we must produce. Productivity is an input/ output relationship.

Please let us address critical issues of electricity, policy environment, education and technology and of course security in order for us to raise the nation's output. However there are even little critical success factors within our reach. The most precious input factor in productivity is time and time management. We parade highest number of public holidays on earth. Some of these holidays legitimize idleness rather than promoting decent work with respect to rest.

The challenge lies in stimulating institutional productivity. At the heart of this institutional productivity is the National Productivity Centre (NPC):

"the need to improve the quantity and quality of goods and services available for consumption in Nigeria as a means of increasing total wealth, is a task to which successive Nigerian Government have attached great importance. Between 1963 and 1985, series of panels and commission were set up by the various governments of Nigeria to work out the modalities for instituting productivity consciousness in the nation's system. The 1963 Morgan Wages Commission and the Okotie-Eboh Tripartite Agreement of 1964 recommended *inter-alia*, the establishment of a National Wage Advisory Council whose function was to advise Government on Wages Policy by keeping watch, not only over trends in wages and price but also in the general development within the economy. However, the Adebo Wages and Salaries Commission of 1970 recommended the setting up of the Productivity, Price and Income Board (PPIB) responsible for establishing a productivity scheme based on the formulation of guidelines on Productivity Improvement.

On its part, the Whitely Council in 1971 recommended the establishment of a Productivity Centre (NPC), while the Udoji Service Review Commission of 1974 stresses the importance of a result oriented public service in addition to stressing the need for increases productivity. The first concrete step to ensure the institution of an organized Productivity Movement in Nigeria was however not taken until 1987. At a jointly organized conference in Ibadan, the Productivity, Prices and Income Board (PPIB), the Nigeria Institute of Social and Economic Research (NISER) and the Federal Ministry of Labour recommended an organized Productivity Movement in Nigeria. This recommendation led to the change of name of the Ministry of Labour in 1979, to Ministry of Employment, Labour and Productivity.

The year, 1979 also saw the lunched of the 4th Development plan, which specially named Increasing Productivity as one of its eleven objectives. Consequently, at the inauguration of the National Productivity Committee by the then Honourable Minister of Labour, all the existing nineteen (19) states were given directives to establish similar Productivity Committees.

In 1984, the National Productivity Centre was formally inaugurated while the enabling Decree No. 7 now (Act CAP 272 of 1994) was promulgated in April, 1987, thus legally establishing the Centre as a federal parastatal. The history of the Centre will be incomplete without highlighting the roles of played by international organizations, such as the International Labour Organization (ILO) and the United Nation Development Programme (UNDP). These two provided the technical as well as financial assistance for the take-off of the Centre."

It should also be on record that President Goodluck Jonathan is the first president to productively sign the Productivity Order of Merit making the point that productivity improvement matters if Nigeria is indeed ready to be part of the leading economies soonest.

Reinventing the Human Resource[*]

Eid Mubarak! Many thanks to the Third Estate Club of Ilorin for mainstreaming human resources in development discourse as part of the 2014 Sallah Dinner lecture. Yours sincerely delivered the lecture.

In his latest book, *My Vision, Challenges In The Race For Excellence*, Sheikh Mohammed bin Rashidi Al Maktoum, the Vice President of the United Arab Emirates (UAE), and constitutional monarch of Dubai observed (and I agree with him) that; "Human beings are the most precious assets of all nations and the most important factors in the progress of countries. We consider the development of human resources as a gauge for the development of our country." I searched in vain for some quotable quotes about human resources from Nigeria's leaders who are currently jostling for political positions. In 2009 there was a dramatic 35% crash in stock prices. There was a mass frenzy to save the market. Trillions of naira was expended by the CBN to rescue and recapitalize six banks in 2010! In 2014, almost 69 per cent of all candidates that sat for West African School Certificate examinations failed to have 5 credits including English and Mathematics! Indeed only 31.2% (i.e.529, 425,000 out of 1,692,435,000 candidates) had credit pass in 5 subjects including English and Mathematics in the 2014 as against a 36.57% in 2013, and 38.81% in 2012. This free fall in the value of present and future human resources has not shocked the nation beyond ordinary. The concluded National Conference of which I was a delegate had 20 sub-committees. I bear witness that the relatively insignificant marginal report on Resource Control of the sub-Committee on Devolution of powers generated more enthusiasm than the reports

[*] Monday October 6th, 2014

207

on say religion or on human resources like Labour, Youth dealing with mass unemployment and mass poverty! Are we saying there is only one resource in Nigeria (oil and gas) and that the problem was how share it or control it through some sharing formulae for oil revenue? According to Minister of Health, Dr Onyebuchi Chukwu, more than 5000 Nigerian trained medical doctors are currently practising in the United States of America! Currently, Nigeria has only 600 paediatricians to care for its over 40 million children compared to the United Kingdom's over 5,000 for 20 million children. Why must we export doctors when we lack them at home? Why are we eager to control oil revenue and remain indifferent to the *New York Times*' report according to which "America Is Stealing the World's Doctors", many of them Nigerians? The formation of Nigeria's human capital is of great importance in the coming years if Nigeria wants to be part of the leading economies in 2020.

According to Human Development Index Nigeria is ranked 156 among 187 countries meaning that Nigeria is considered to have low level of human development. The National Commission for Non-formal and Mass Education Commission (NCNME) just revealed that as many as 64 million Nigerian adults are illiterates! This is a shame turned tragedy. Countries with less endowment like Zimbabwe and Cuba had archived literacy rates of 90.70% and 99.9% respectively. Why would the world's 13th oil producing nation that Nigeria is slide back into mass ignorance and underdevelopment. Local government edits and state laws must make primary schooling compulsory and criminalize and penalize parents that do not allow their wards to go schools in the 21st century. To appreciate human resource we must motivate the labour which constitutes the great resource. We must ensure workers are paid well and on time. It should be noted that delay of salary is the same as wage theft. The national Minimum wage is due for a review next year. The 2010 National Tripartite Committee on National Minimum Wage headed by Justice S.M.A. Belgore, GCON, recommended that to avoid ad-hoc approach, the minimum wage is supposed to be reviewed every 5years. It is due this year! Time to review this is NOW!

We must also institute a system of reward and discipline to motivate labour for development. I commend President Goodluck

208

Jonathan for the recent national honour award and recognition of the designer of Nigerian Flag, Mr Taiwo Akinkunmi after years of neglect and his employment as a Special Assistant, with a salary for life. Indeed the President is further encouraged to pay his arrears since 1960 he designed Nigerian flag. We must move from jobless to job-led growth. We must reinvent the real sector of the economy, revive labour intensive industries and get the army of unemployed working. We must improve on productivity. In 1958, late Ahmadu Bello said that: "My motto for the newborn North is "Work and worship". We should not consume what we do not produce; stop exporting what we should add value to.

There are even little critical success factors within our immediate reach. The most precious input factor in productivity is time and time management. We parade highest number of public holidays on earth. Some of these holidays legitimize idleness rather than promoting decent work with respect to rest. How on earth do you declare a free working day to "mark" Democracy Day, a day arbitrarily chosen by one man in office that could even fall on a Monday? Why would children not be in schools on a Monday in the name of democracy? To deepen and defend democracy, we must work and work, read and read, not just idle away. Nigeria works 8 hrs, 5 days a week. But on average, other 19 countries in our preferred club of 20 most developed countries, (come the magic 2020!) work longer hours, 6 days a week. Out of 365 days in a year, Nigeria is at rest for some 120 days. Out of the official 8 hrs, we resume unofficially at 10 am, set to do some unofficial school (children) runs by noon, only to unofficially close shops at 3 pm ostensibly to beat the traffic.

Index

Abacha, General Sani; 22, 28, 39, 40, 43, 56, 107
Abdullahi, Colonel Ahmed; 3
Abubakar, Abdulsalami; 38, 41
Abubakar, Umar Munir; 127
Abubakar, Vice President Atiku; 81
Academic Staff Union of Universities (ASUU); 38, 150, 151, 184, 185
Adebo Wages and Salaries Commission of 1970; 205
Adeniyi, Olusegun; 83, 85
AFL-CIO; 75
Africa's productivity problem; 18
African National Congress (ANC); 134
African Trade Union Confederation (ATUC); 170
African Union (AU); 46
Aganga, Dr. Olusegun; 139
Agbede, Prof. I.O.; 152
Agbese, Dan; 7
Ahmad, Muhammad K; 125, 146, 160
Ahmed, Alhaji Mahmud Yayale; 111
Ahmed, Alhaji Uba; 21, 27
Aji, Dr. Abba; 52
Akanbi Commission; 54
Ake, Wilson; 108
Akhigbe, Governor Mike; 5
Akinkunmi, Taiwo; 209
Akumu, Denis; 170
All-African Trade Union Federation (AATUF); 170
Amending the Pension Act 2013 (PRA13); 177
Ani, Chief Anthony; 30
Asobie, Professor Assisi; 152
Audu, Honourable Ado Dogo; 108
Augulana, Reginald; 140

Awolowo, Chief Obafemi; 37, 169
Awute, L.N. ; 201
Awuzie, Professor Ukachukwu; 151
Azikiwe, Dr. Nnamdi; 1, 169
Bafyau, Paschal; 36, 37, 120, 141
Balewa, Alhaji Sir Tafawa; 82
Bande, Professor Tijani Mohammed; 187
Bank of Industry (BOI); 68, 137, 141, 156
Bdliya, Dr Paul; 204
Beckman, Bjorn; 55, 79, 142
Belgore, Hon Justice S. M. A.; 111, 112, 208
Bello, Ahmadu; 209
Belounis, Zahir; 195·
British TUC; 75
Brown, Gordon; 195
Bur, Ason; 12
Burrow, Sharan; 194
Canadian Labour Congress (CLC); 80
Castro, Fidel; 45, 69, 70
Central Organisation of Trade Unions COTU (Kenya); 170
Chidok, Osita; 204
Chiroma, Alhaji Ali; 26, 38, 120, 141
Chukwu, Dr Onyebuchi; 208
Civil Service Technical Workers' Union; 6
Civil Service Union (1912); 118, 153, 154
Consolidated Medical Salary Scale (CONMESS); 148
Council of South African Trade Unions (COSATU); 80
Crisis of compensation; 14
Dabibi, Milton; 38
Dangote, Alhaji Aliko; 138
Danjuma, Lt. General Theophilus; 53
Decent Work Agenda (DWA); 86, 87, 147
Declaration of Philadelphia in 1944; 174
Diori, Hamani; 169
Doctors' sack - end of Decent Work; 147
ECOWAS; 47
Elliott, Larry; 195
Employees Compensation Act of 2010; 109, 126
End of work; 30, 63
Essien, Chief Effiong; 5

Etok, Senator Aloysius; 178
European Union (EU); 75
Fafowora, Dr Dapo; 2
Falae, Chief Olu; 44
Fashina, Dr. Dipo; 151, 152
Fayemi, Kayode; 115
Foreign Exchange Market (FEM, SFEM); 1-3
Friedrich Ebert Stiftung (FES); 137, 141
Fuel price protest; 133
Full-time-part-time issue; 23
Ghana Trades Union Congress; 170
Ghosh, Jayati; 195
Goni, Alhaji Bukar; 204
Governor, Chief Akande; 37
Gusau, Ahmed; 41
Human recapitalisation; 66
Ibrahim Babangida administration; 26
Iganmu, Mr. Ibrahim; 139
Ige, Chief Bola; 37
ILO Conventions No. 87 and 98; 88, 182, 186
IMF and World anti-labour policy advice; 48, 72
Imo formula; 6, 11, 12
Imoudu, Pa Michael; 169
Independent Petroleum Marketers Association of Nigeria (IPMAN); 193
Industrial Arbitration Panel (IAP); 148, 193
Inienger, Colonel John; 3
Institute of Registered Safety Professional Bill of 2010; 108
International Confederation of Free Trade Unions – Africa Regional
    Organisation (ICFTU-AFRO); 45
International Labour Organization (ILO); 41, 44, 45, 47, 50, 70, 94, 105-
    107, 111, 125, 173-176, 180, 189
International Monetary Fund (IMF); 70, 72
International Textile and Garment Workers' Federation; 142
International Trade Union Congress (ITUC); 80, 154, 194, 196
Iwu, Professor Maurice; 81, 82
Iyayi, Professor Festus; 152
Jega, Professor Attahiru; 120, 152
Jeyifo, Prof. Biodun; 152
John Olarewaju; 86

Jonathan, President Goodluck; 111, 112, 115, 122, 125, 127, 129, 145, 146, 159, 163, 164, 168, 188, 198, 200, 201, 204, 206, 208-209
Jubril, Senator Walid; 140
Kale, Dr. Yemi; 191
Kano, Mallam Aminu; 169
Kaunda, Kenneth; 169
Kazeem, Comrade Adebayo; 40
Keita, Modibo; 169
Kirkland, Lane; 79
Kokori, Chief Frank; 21, 23, 38
"Kwara Formula"; 12
Labour Act of 1974; 11
Labour Advisory Council (LAC); 27
Labour and democratic process; 55
Labour and development; 38, 45
Labour as Endangered Species; 102
Labour Party (LP); 80, 81
Lech Walesa's Solidarity Movement; 71
Life after work; 50
Lukman, Rilwanu; 3
Madiba; 65
Maina, AbdulRasheed; 144, 159, 160, 162-164
Maku, Labaran; 138
Mamman, Mallam Yusuf; 9
Mandela, Nelson; 69, 115
Manufacturers' Association of Nigeria (MAN); 2
Mark, Governor (Senator) David; 6, 11, 162, 163
Mboya, Tom; 169
Michael Imoudu National Institute for Labour Studies (MINILS); 86
Millennium Development Goals (MDGs); 192
Mimiko, Olusegun; 121
Minimum wage; 111
Mohammed, Dr. Rufai; 52
Mohammed, Salisu; 27
Morgan Wages Commission 1963; 205
Muhammed, General Murtala; 43
Muhammed, President Comrade Kiri; 153, 155
Musa, Balarabe; 43
Naidoo, Jay; 195
National Directorate of Employment (NDE); 141

National Economic Empowerment and Development Strategy (NEEDS); 64

National Examination Council (NECO); 129, 132

National Industrial Court (NIC); 149, 193

National Institute of Policy and Strategic Studies, (NIPPS); 187

National Labour Advisory Council (NLAC); 193

National Minimum Wage Bill of 2010; 112

National Minimum Wage Order of 1986; 6

National Pension Commission (PENCOM); 60, 76-78, 125, 141, 160, 161, 163, 164, 179, 198, 199, 200

National Productivity Centre (NPC); 19, 141, 205

National Productivity Day (NPD); 204

National Provident Fund (NPF); 52

National Social Insurance Trust Fund (NSITF); 52, 53, 60, 61, 108-110, 127, 141

National Union of Pensioners, (NUP); 162

National Union of Petroleum and Gas Workers (NUPENG); 21, 23, 26, 38, 106

National Union of Teachers (NUT); 91, 131, 154

National Union of Textile, Garment and Tailoring Workers (NUTGWN); 136, 140-143

NEPAD, 46, 47

New Employee Compensation Act (ECA); 125

"Niger Formula"; 12

Nigeria Civil Service Union (NCSU); 153

Nigeria Employers Consultative Association (NECA); 127, 193

Nigeria Immigration Service (NIS); 94

Nigeria Institute for Social and Economic Research (NISER); 111

Nigeria Labour Congress (NLC); 6-10, 13, 19, 26, 28, 36, 38, 39, 41, 44, 45, 55-57, 73, 80, 84, 85, 92, 100, 106, 110, 111, 118-122, 127, 133-136, 142, 154, 156, 163, 166, 167, 174, 178, 193

Nigeria Medical Association (NMA); 201

Nigeria Textile Manufacturers Association; 139, 140

Nigeria Union of Railway Workers (NURW); 56, 154, 184

Nkrumah, Kwame; 169

Non-Academic Staff Union (NASU); 38

Nyerere, Julius; 116

OAU/AU Labour and Social Affairs Commission; 171

Obasanjo, President; 36, 39, 43, 44, 70, 71, 81, 82, 84, 125, 145, 192

Ofeimun, Odia; 1

Ogundimu, Dr. B.A.; 152
Okogie, Archbishop; 36
Okonjo-Iweala, Ngozi; 63, 64, 68
Okotie-Eboh Tripartite Agreement of 1964; 205
Okpala, Professor Promise; 129
Olarewaju, John P.; 139
Olejeme, Ngozi; 127
Omar, Comrade Abdulwaheed; 84, 119, 122, 140, 141, 167, 193
Onabanjo, Chief Bisi; 8
Onabanjo, Chief Bisi; 8
Onaran, Professor Ozlem; 195
Oni, Segun; 115
Organization of African Trade Union Unity (OATUU); 80, 121, 122, 154,
    169-171, 173
Organization of African Unity (OAU); 170
Oronsaye, Steve; 115
Oshiomhole, Adams; 44, 51, 85, 120, 121, 138, 141, 187
Otobo, Professor Dafe; 153
Ouaddou, Abdeslam ; 195
Pa Imoudu; 38
Pan-African Workers' Congress; 170
Party for Social Democracy (PSD); 80
Pay cut or pay equity; 98
Pedro, Deputy Governor Femi; 82
PENGASSAN; 38, 106
Pension fraud; 144
Pension Reform Act of 2004; 59, 137, 146, 159, 161, 168, 177
Pension Reform Bill 2014; 200
Pension, beyond verification; 76
Pensions Act of 1979; 53-62, 146, 168, 178
Pope John Paul II; 69, 70
Poverty Reduction Strategy Paper (PRSP); 48, 49, 67
Presidential Pension Reform Task Team, (PRTT); 144, 159, 163
Productivity Awareness Day; 18
Productivity, Prices and Incomes Board (PPIB); 2
Re-inventing decent mass employment; 86
Reinventing human resource; 207
Restoring trade union independence; 26
Rethinking doctors mass sack; 201
Rethinking labour; 72, 156

Rethinking the Senate Constitution Amendment on Labour; 180
Revenue Mobilization, Allocation and Fiscal Commission; 98
Rimi, Abubakar; 43
Rufa'i, Professor Ruqayyatu Ahmed; 130
Ryder, Guy; 173, 194
Sambo, Arch. Namadi; 139, 204
Sanusi, Sanusi Lamido; 155, 188
Saraki, Governor Bukola; 92
Saving pensioners; 166
Shabalala, Thambo; 142
Shagari, President Shehu; 43
Sogolo, Godwin; 8-10
Soludo, Charles; 66
Sommer, Michael; 194
Strike as acid; 83
Structural Adjustment Programme (SAP); 1-7, 14, 18-20, 67, 131, 157, 171
Sule-Kano, Dr. Abdullahi; 152
Sunmonu, Alhaji Hassan; 36, 119, 141, 170, 172
Sylva, Governor P.; 121
Teachers' strike; 90
Tinubu, Governor Bola; 82
Toure, Ahmed Sekou; 169
Trade Union Ordinance of 1930s; 71
TUC; 84, 85, 111, 122, 133
Tukur, Dr. Mahmud M.; 152
Udogu, Dr Emmanuel; 40
Udoji Service Review Commission of 1974; 205
Uduaghan, Dr. Emmanuel; 138
Umoh, James Umoh; 6
Union Makes Us Strong; 136
United Nations Development Programme (UNDP); 50, 66, 67, 194
United Nations Industrial Development Organisation (UNIDO); 103, 104, 137
United Nations Millennium Development Goals (MDGs); 66
Universal Basic Education (UBE); 131
Utomi, Pat; 8, 10
Utuama, Professor Amos; 140
Vision 2020; 32, 123
Wage Crisis; 34
West African Examinations Council (WAEC); 130, 132

What about industrial relations?; 187
Wike, Barrister Nyesom; 130
Williams, Chief Rotimi; 69, 70
Wogu, Chief Emeka; 138, 140, 193, 204
Workmen Compensation Act (WCA) of 1987; 109, 126
Workmen Compensation Bill of 2010; 108
Workmen Compensation Ordinance of 1942; 109
Workplace Safety and Health Bill 2010; 108
World Bank; 70
World Development Report of 1995; 20
World pension summit; 198
Yakowa, Patrick Ibrahim; 140
Yar'Adua, President Umar; 82-84, 87, 91, 92, 96, 102, 111, 145, 188
Yaro, Alhaji Mukhtar; 140

Printed in the United States
By Bookmasters